TWO UNLIKELY PEOPLE TO CHANGE THE WORLD

A Memoir by **KAREN BERG**

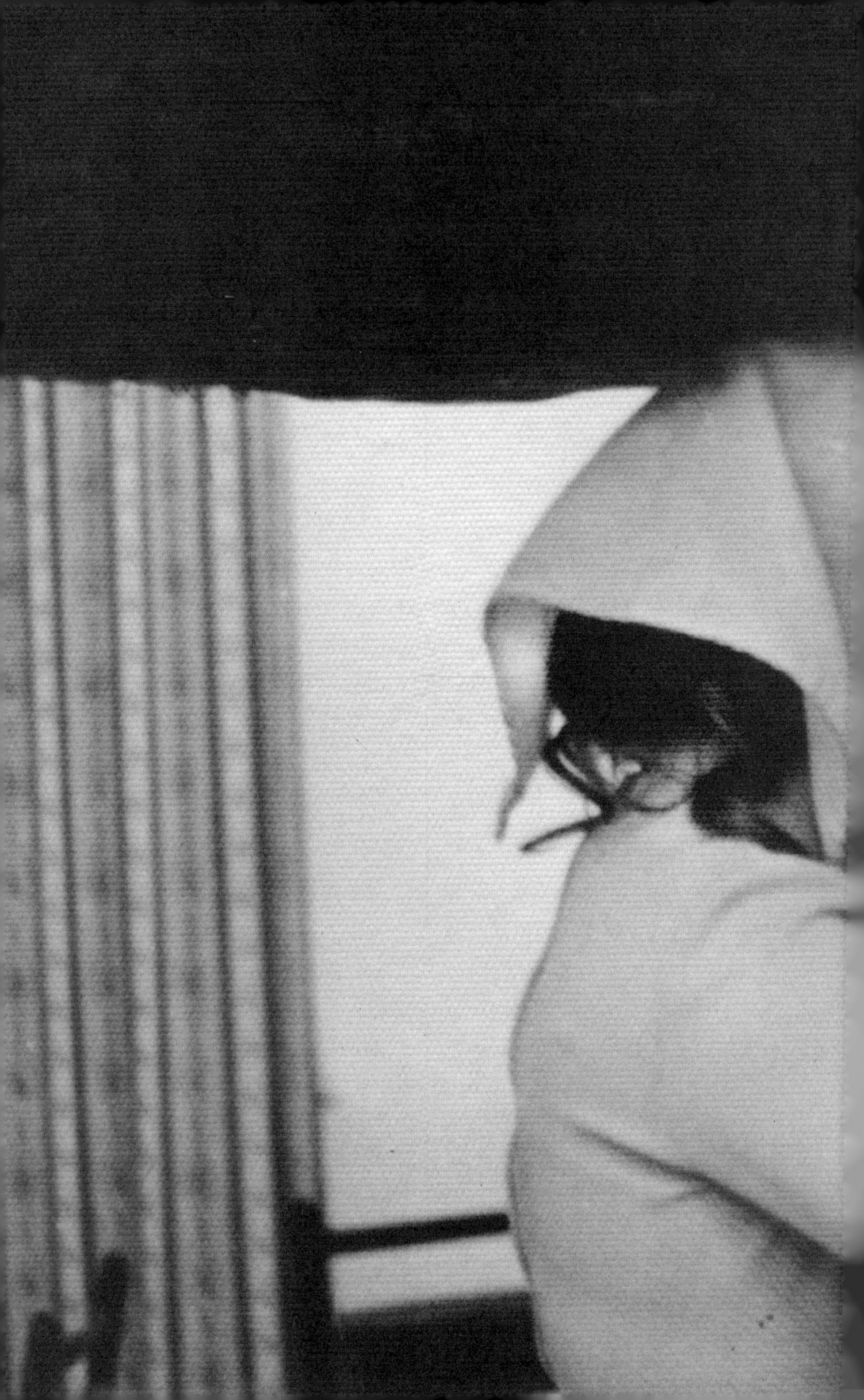

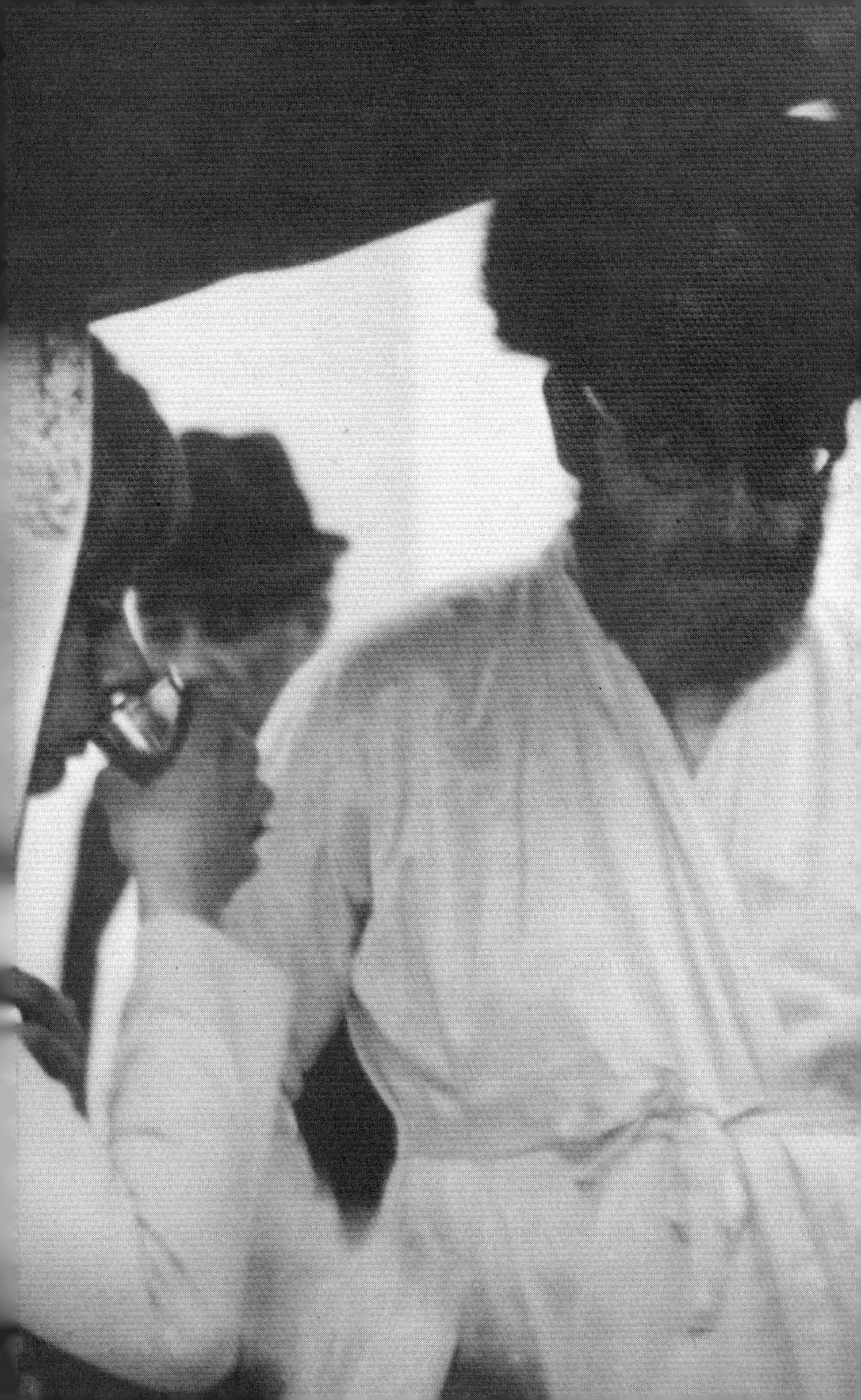

Kabbalah Centre Publishing is a registered DBA of Kabbalah Centre International, Inc.

For further information:

The Kabbalah Centre
155 E. 48th St., New York, NY 10017
1062 S. Robertson Blvd., Los Angeles, CA 90035

1.800.Kabbalah www.kabbalah.com

Printed in Canada, August 2019

Hardcover ISBN: 978-1-57189-992-7
Paperback ISBN: 978-1-57189-993-4

Design: HL Design (Hyun Min Lee) www.hldesignco.com

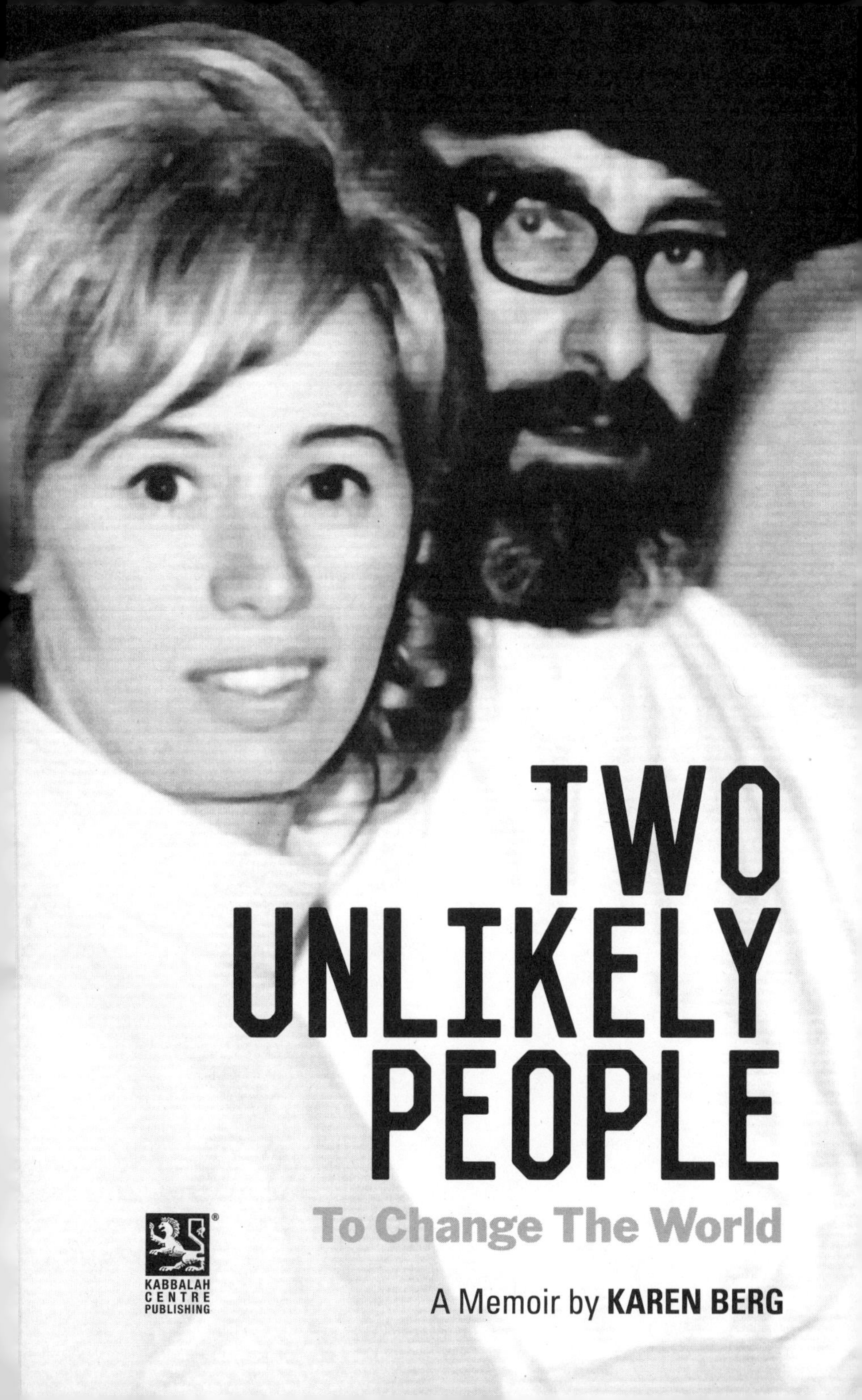

TWO UNLIKELY PEOPLE

To Change The World

A Memoir by **KAREN BERG**

השער לה' צדיקים יבאו בו

Acknowledgments

This book has been such an important passage for me; it has granted me the rare occasion to pause and look back while running forward with all my strength. Its writing would not have been possible without the help of writer and editor, Susan Golant. For those of you who know me, the thought that I would sit for three years in front of a computer is about as likely as me flying to the moon. Susan helped me capture the Rav's story, my own, and the honest account of the creation of the Kabbalah Centre. It took thousands of pages of interviews, historical research, and plenty of writing and rewriting for her to help me find my voice.

A project like this, while it appears to carry my name, does not belong to any one person: It belongs to all those who shared the experiences they had with the Rav, to those who remembered things I didn't, to those who researched and found articles and lessons the Rav taught. It belongs to a global community of dedicated people who accepted the unlikely pair of the Rav and I and what was created through us.

Rav, you always have and still do fill every part of my being with purpose, with love, with life. Loving you and being your partner was my destiny and blessing.

To my children, you often paid for the decisions we made. Living a life shaped by a destiny to serve the world does not always make for a warm and secure childhood. Yet you accepted the story set before you, as hard as it was, with grace. Thank you for sharing the journey. I love you all so much and am appreciative of the people you have become.

To the Chevre, thank you for your commitment and for your desire to make this path your own. The Kabbalah Centre would not have been able to do the good that it has in the world without the group called the Chevre who strive to live the wisdom and be of service to humanity. Thank you to the staff, donors, and volunteers who share their talent, their time and their financial support so that others can learn this life-enriching wisdom and so we can turn on the lights every day.

To everyone who has shared their energy in whatever way in the pages of this book and to the history that it recounted, please accept my humble gratitude.

TABLE OF CONTENTS

Foreword

This is not a traditional biography with a chronological enumeration of dates and places and events, because my husband's was not a traditional existence. Interwoven with details of his life and our life together, you will find a memoir of lessons he taught and ideas he was most fervent about. His every thought and action were part of a larger whole—a profound knowledge of the universe that Philip Berg, who later became known as the Rav, acquired and then imparted. As his wife, I look back in these pages on our lives together, and I'm reminded of salient moments that defined his character and destiny. I include here events that are representative of his passion and purpose—events that also shaped my own journey, our tumultuous marriage, and the creation of the worldwide network known as the Kabbalah Centre. Besides, it's not in my nature to be strictly linear.

While this is not a book about the principles of Kabbalah, it is impossible to separate the man from the wisdom and the wisdom from the man. One of the central themes in the Rav's life and Kabbalah is love—the love of every person, no matter their religious upbringing or deeds. Indeed, my husband eventually came to recognize that despite the fact that it had arisen from centuries of Jewish mystical thought, Kabbalah is for everyone regardless of their faith. And even though he was loving toward all, he was far from soft.

For the most part, his was a demanding kind of love—one that asked others to step up. He would not censor himself if he saw that someone was being spiritually dishonest, and so to some he came off as challenging and even harsh. At other times, however, he was kind—especially if he sensed that a person was in great need of support. It is fair to say that he embodied both the tough and gentle sides of love. He also knew only one way to be: completely transparent and utterly truthful.

In many ways the Rav's life was not his own. Rather, it was a path set out for him as part of a lineage. In fact, the Rav and I did not have what most people would consider a personal life—one that contained separate compartments for home, work, family, and friends. Instead, ours was a tapestry of many experiences sewn into one all-encompassing whole, framed by our relentless mutual desire to bring the Light and consciousness into this world, and by doing so to help people to improve their life and destiny.

* * *

The Bible portion Baha'alotcha explains that throughout their wanderings in the wilderness, the Israelites were led by the Cloud of Glory. Their journey was dictated by divine providence. This may sound inspiring and wonderful but like all connections with the Light in this physical world, it came with a price. The people were not asked where they wished to travel or whether or not they wished to stay in any one place. Rather, they dutifully followed the Cloud. Wherever it settled, they camped; whenever it departed, they followed.

Sometimes the region was unpleasant, yet the Cloud would remain. Sometimes the Israelites were led to an oasis with good water and cooling shade but the Cloud would not linger. They never knew the length of any stay. They might have just unpacked and settled in when suddenly the Cloud would direct them that it was time to go. The Israelites traveled this way for forty years. And in that time they journeyed through 42 stations, which are considered to be the 42 stages of life. At each location, the Israelites were presented with a challenge requiring them to make a spiritual choice.

My life with the Rav (which incidentally lasted 42 years from 1971 – 2013) was much like that of the people of the wilderness. We never knew where we would be called to go, how long we would stay, or what adventures would find us along the way, nevertheless that was how we lived. That was who the Rav was, that's the way he wanted it, and it suited me just fine.

הישיבה הקדושה
ללימוד תורת הנסתר
מראות הסולם
רבנו יהודה ליב הלוי אשלג

CHAPTER 1:

SHRAGA FEIVEL GRUBERGER: THE EARLY YEARS

It has been written that each of our lives contains a paradox: our destiny is already known to the Creator but we have the power and free will to alter it. Whether we do so in this lifetime or in future incarnations is a choice each of us must make. Philip Berg, my husband the Rav, altered his life radically and fulfilled a destiny he might never have imagined for himself. From his modest beginnings as the youngest child in a poor, immigrant family, he became a powerful businessman who then transformed yet again into a spiritual force of nature.

The Rav was the first man in history to popularize the ancient wisdom of Kabbalah by spreading it in every direction, to all people—men and women, Jews and non-Jews. His tenacity, force of will, and teachings filled a curriculum, supported teachers, and fostered spiritual connections that led to the creation of more than forty Kabbalah Centres in the world. They continue to contribute to the life of cities such as New York, London, Paris, Johannesburg, Mexico City, Moscow, San Paolo, Sydney, Hong Kong, and Manila among others.

Through the Rav's tireless efforts and singular, laser-focus vision, the wisdom of Kabbalah has reached millions. The path was strewn with formidable obstacles, as you will see, but as his revered teacher, Rav Yehuda Tzvi Brandwein once told the Rav, "Your gift and your duty is to explain Kabbalah in such a way that all people will easily understand." This he did with certainty, with every fiber of his being, and with great fullness of heart.

* * *

Shraga Feivel Gruberger entered this world on August 20, 1927 in Brooklyn, New York. His parents, Esther and Max Gruberger arrived from Stanislav, Poland with their eldest son, as part of the great tide of immigrants who came to these shores after World War I, before the Great Depression. The family descended from observant Jews living in central Europe—Austria and Hungary, with a little bit of Russia and the Ukraine thrown in. They were "*Galitzianer*," members of the Ashkenazi branch of European Jews who originated in the region of Galicia. At one time, the area was a royal province of the Austro-Hungarian empire, although political borders in that part of Europe shifted frequently.

An entire culture sprang up around being a *Galitzianer*. The Jews of Galicia lived modestly. Most worked as craftsmen, tailors, milliners, carpenters, machinists, wholesale and retail traders, and jewelers in small workshops and businesses. They had a strong bias toward education, believing that it would help them move forward in society. Many eventually became doctors and dentists. Their rivals were Jews from Lithuania, the so-called *Litvaks*. *Galitzianers* tended to be more Chassidic, more soulful, and more prayerful than the Litvaks, who in turn regarded them disdainfully as irrational and uneducated. Polish Jews could easily distinguish one group from the other by their Yiddish pronunciation and their eating habits. Galician Jews generally had a sweet tooth and a habit of adding sugar to their gefilte fish—one of my husband's favorite foods!

When the Grubergers arrived in New York, they naturally gravitated toward *Galitzianer* enclaves in the Williamsburg section of Brooklyn, where they found synagogues, yeshivas, shops, and a social circle that felt comfortable and familiar. Religious Jews who came to the United States in those years were Orthodox but moderate in their views. For instance, men and women were not kept separate during a wedding, which is common practice for ultra-Orthodox Jews. Nor did that generation dress in long robes or fur hats, with the exception of a few grand Chassidic rabbis. Max Gruberger, the Rav's father, wore a gartle or belt around his waist during prayer (as did the Rav until the 1980s), but otherwise the community was relatively modern and open.

In the 1930s and 40s persecuted Jews of various Chassidic sects like the Lubavitchers or the Satmars had not yet emigrated to New York from Hungary and Romania, bringing with them a wave of ultra-Orthodoxy.

The Chassids never shaved their beards and they grew long sidelocks (*peyois*), but photos of Max and Esther show him clean shaven and in modern garb—a hat and suit. The Grubergers were observant Jews but not ultra-Orthodox, more what I think of as "Chassid-ish."

At that time, Williamsburg was also home to newly-arrived Irish and Italian families who lived in close proximity to the Jews. In fact, the whole neighborhood was teeming with immigrants, doubling its population between 1900 and 1920. By 1917, this community was the most densely packed in all of New York—one block near where the Grubergers lived between South 2nd Street and South 3rd Street, housed more than 5,000 people—and as far as my husband knew, no one else existed in the world.

The Rav was born two years before the great stock market crash of 1929 that would leave millions of people jobless, homeless, and penniless. Although my husband never spoke of how the Depression impacted him and his family, its influence was clear in his care to find small savings and to never be wasteful. In fact, the Rav was frugal beyond what most people would consider normal. He always reminded members of the Centre to turn off the lights when we left a room. When we needed something, he wanted us to research costs and go with the cheapest price, even if it didn't always make sense.

When it came to our books, he would negotiate with printers down to the penny, sometimes ordering larger print runs than we needed because the cost per book was a few cents less. And there were times when I pushed to purchase certain buildings for the Centre, but he would fight me all the way, unhappy with a mortgage that put us in debt. Although he had been a successful businessman, he was extremely conservative when it came to spending.

The Gruberger family eventually took up residence in a small five-story, walk-up, brick apartment building with scrolled window cornices and a typical front stoop at 159 South 2nd Street, near Bedford Avenue in Brooklyn, only four or five blocks from the East River and three blocks from the Williamsburg Bridge. The building, constructed in 1907, contained roughly two dozen apartments and was situated next to an old fire station. As was the custom in those days, fire escapes zigzagged the façade of the building. Here residents slept outside on steamy summer nights, and laundry lines were strung like colorfully festooned cobwebs.

Inside, the apartments were far from grand. A typical two-bedroom measured only 700 square feet, so the five Grubergers—including the Rav's older brothers, Oscar and Sigmund—squeezed into tight quarters. Rather than being constructed in the old-fashioned railroad car design, with one room opening into the next, their apartment had a more modern central hallway. In today's market such an apartment could cost north of a million dollars, but in 1940, when the Rav was 13, his parents paid $29.00 a month in rent. Their neighbors included many families in the same socio-economic group, mostly newly arrived Jewish immigrants from Eastern Europe with some children born in the old country and some in the United States.

Since this was largely a Jewish neighborhood, nearby shops would have included the Kosher butcher, where freshly plucked chickens hung by their necks on hooks in the windows, great slabs of brisket, calf's liver, and beef tongue gleamed in refrigerated cases, and sawdust littered the floor. On Friday mornings, the air would have been redolent with the aroma of baking challahs, Mandelbrot, and twisted chocolate cinnamon babkas. Fishmongers put out large tin basins with live carp and pike, ready to be stunned with a blow to the head, wrapped in newspaper, and sent home to be gutted and cleaned for the first course of the evening meal.

Housewives darted in and out of greengrocers' shops whose wares spilled out to the street, their mesh shopping bags bulging with the onions, potatoes, carrots, and apples they'd haggled to buy for Shabbat dinner. In the afternoon, the pungent aromas of simmering chicken soup, sweet gefilte fish, and chulent (a dense beef, barley, and potato stew) filled the air with anticipation as the men hurried home from work or yeshiva in time to prepare for the evening's rituals. The Rav had a particular fondness for potato kugel made with grated potatoes, eggs, onions, and flour, which his mother used to bake for Shabbat dinners.

Esther Gruberger was a housewife and a loving parent. She was a righteous woman too. Every Shabbat afternoon she would be found at home, following the Chassidic custom of reading the entire Book of Psalms. She was short, and in her later years, quite overweight. Although I never met her, I knew he and his mother were close. He described how she would bring a hot lunch for him to the yeshiva even when he was in high school. Although his dad was at work most of the time, his mother was home both before and after school, caring for her children. Whenever he talked about her, the Rav expressed great warmth. For his father he had reverence, but not the same tenderness.

As a young man, Max Gruberger was conscripted as a cook in the Russian army during World War I. He was a tall, thin man of few words—a hard worker and a kind person. As far as I know, he had no formal education, though like most Jews he was fluent in Yiddish and Hebrew and could read the Torah. Although we don't know what profession he held in Poland, once in New York he became a presser in the garment business. My husband used to speak of "walking the bridge" in blazing sun and frigid winds—that is, crossing the East River on foot over the Williamsburg Bridge as he and his father made their way to the Lower East Side of Manhattan. Here countless sweatshops and factories had been established, often on the upper floors of tenement apartment buildings.

My husband's oldest brother, Oscar, thirteen years his senior, worked as a presser as well. These men had difficult jobs, lifting irons that weighed as much as 20 pounds to finish the garments that their co-workers had stitched together. This was hot work during the winter as the men toiled with the steam irons in small spaces with closed, barred windows. In the summer it was blistering. It was also unpredictable. During the high season, bosses forced their workers to labor for long hours to meet increased demand, while the slow season found many garment workers unemployed.

The Grubergers didn't want this kind of life for their youngest son. Although they were not Chassidim in the strict sense of the word, they still closely followed Orthodox Jewish traditions, if not the letter of the law. So they put little Shraga into a religious elementary school at the age of three, in hopes that eventually he would become a rabbi or learned man. They did everything possible to make this experience enjoyable for him. The family lived across the street from the primary school *cheder*, allowing their young son to come home for lunch between classes. After school, there was always chocolate and a glass of milk waiting for him. My husband's formidable Galitzianer sweet tooth survived his childhood. At home, he would ask for dessert—especially pareve ice cream—at the Friday table, knowing full well it was detrimental to his health. When I said as much, he would go to the freezer and take it out and eat it anyway.

* * *

The Rav's Bar Mitzvah date fell on the week that the Bible portion Deuteronomy 11:26–16:17 is read. I find this prophetic, given that the first word and the name of the portion, "Re'eh," means "to see." This is the longest portion in Deuteronomy, but interestingly it is one of the few that isn't explicated in the Zohar (the kabbalistic interpretation of the Bible, the Five Books of Moses). Instead, its meaning is concealed.

The portion Re'eh begins with Moses telling the people of Israel, "See, I place before you today a blessing and a curse." The blessing will come when the Israelites fulfill the Creator's commandments, but they will be cursed if they abandon them. Moses then goes on to enumerate the Creator's decrees, which include the building of a Temple on a site of the Creator's choosing; the shunning of idolatry and human sacrifice; the destruction of communities that worshipped false prophets; the rules governing kashrut (kosher food); and the importance of tithing and charity.

Why do I say this Bar Mitzvah reading is prophetic? As I mentioned, the word re'eh means "to see." As the Rav used to say, Kabbalah is the study of the seen and the unseen dimensions; it is a quest to understand the inner workings of the universe. Kabbalists believe that we only see 1% of reality, the physical world; the other 99%, the spiritual world, is invisible to us. Thanks to the Rav and his lineage of teachers we have Kabbalah to help us see what our eyes cannot: the metaphysical realms that lie beyond the reach of our five senses.

The Rav's work, which today continues posthumously through his writings and spiritual teachings, is devoted to making us aware of these hidden dimensions, and to gain access to their unlimited blessings. We tend to think that all of our problems and good fortune stem from the physical realm but this world is just the "playing field of Satan"—one of the Rav's favorite expressions for describing the dwelling place of the oppositional force that challenges us. Kabbalists see darkness as more than just the absence of light; it's a negative energy that actively seeks to wreak havoc, sow confusion, and distract us from the truth. Satan is the name for this force. It is also referred to as the adversary or the opponent.

More is concealed than our eyes will ever behold. The wisdom of Kabbalah helps us to awaken our consciousness in order to explore this hidden spiritual dimension. Kabbalah is based on the notion that there are three primary forces at work in this world, which are described as Columns. On the Right, is the positive force of sharing, and on the Left, the negative energy of receiving. Between them lies the Central Column. Like the filament in a light bulb, it serves as the resistance—or mediating force—that bridges the positive and negative poles in order to manifest the Light of the Creator. We create the Central Column by exercising our free will.

I believe that the heart of the Rav's life story is found in this Bible portion about seeing—from the traditional religious life he was born into, with all of its rules and explications, to the Rav's chosen path of endlessly searching for understanding beyond tradition. The Rav's portion was Re'eh because his ultimate role was to reveal what was hidden; to help us all see and access the beauty and intelligence of the spiritual structure that lies beyond the confines of this limited physical plane, so that humanity could live its purpose to be the "determinator," as the Rav used to say. It is in in our hands to become the cause of change, to bring about a reality in which "Love Thy Neighbor" is the norm, and chaos, destruction, and death are eliminated from the landscape of this world. I believe, as did the Rav's teacher, that it was his destiny to introduce all people—not just a select few—to Kabbalah's teachings.

My husband possessed an unquenchable desire for knowledge of this spiritual dimension and its impact. The more he studied, the clearer it became, and with this clarity came certainty about the Light of the Creator and the wisdom of Kabbalah. He attained both a scholarly and an intuitive understanding of these aspects of spirit. He was not about following rules blindly, but rather it was his chosen work to do whatever was required to make that which is unseen seen. It was his job to help humanity use the spiritual tools of Kabbalah to raise itself out of a limited reality and discover a boundless source of Light. His purpose in the world was to awaken consciousness and bring about physical immortality, as lofty as that sounds.

* * *

However, none of this was anywhere in evidence during the early part of my husband's life. Kabbalah training lay many years in the future. Instead, Shraga Feivel Gruberger had a much more traditional religious education, which would serve him well later on. My husband's schooling was thorough and formidable, and took place in several different Judaic institutions. Through elementary and high school, he attended Brooklyn's Yeshiva Torah

Vodaas, sometimes referred to as the "mother of American yeshivas." In this venerable institution, founded in 1917, he received an Orthodox education. His religious studies were taught in Hebrew and Aramaic, as well as Yiddish.

In 1946, the Rav spent a year studying at Beth Medrash Govoha in Lakewood, New Jersey. This yeshiva, recently founded by the preeminent Rabbi Aharon Kotler, had sent out a request to other yeshivas in the Greater New York area to send it some of their better students. When the school year came to a close, Shraga returned to Yeshiva Torah Vodaas to complete his education, and finally concluded his religious education by attending Beit Midrash Elyon in Monsey, New York, the post-graduate wing of Yeshiva Torah Vodaas. It was considered an elite educational institution during the 1950s and 1960s. There he received his Rabbinic degree and ordination in late 1951.

During his lengthy, intensive education, my husband studied the Torah (the Five Books of Moses and the Oral Torah) and the Talmud. The Talmud (which means "instruction" in Hebrew) is made up of 63 books or "tractates" that run to more than 6,000 pages in all. This massive compendium of the teachings of thousands of rabbis dates from before the Common Era to the 5th century CE. Among other topics, it covers Jewish ethics, philosophy, customs, history, and folklore, and is the basis for all Jewish law. These 63 books can be divided into two sections: the Mishnah, a written compilation of the Oral Torah—all of the laws, statutes, and legal interpretations that were not part of the original Five Books of Moses and the Gemara (written around the 5th century CE), which is an explanation and expansion of the Mishnah. My husband also studied Midrash—an anthology of thousands of interpretations of passages in the Bible, rabbinic sermons, explications, commentaries, and homilies.

To help support his family, when the Rav was in high school he used to take a horse and wagon out to Canarsie on Jamaica Bay. The area was mostly a swamp at that time. He cut the long reeds that grew in the marsh, piled them up in the wagon, and took them home to sell to neighbors for their Sukkah, the temporary structures used to celebrate the holiday of Sukkot. An old friend of his told me that in 1947, the Rav also sold sweaters that his father had brought home from the Garment District to his classmates for $2.00 apiece.

After his ordination as a rabbi in 1951, the Rav started teaching basic Torah to elementary school age children at a nearby yeshiva in Monsey, New York, which was common practice for young rabbis. At about this time, he married his first wife Rivka Brandwein. As was typical in their social circle, her parents paid a small fortune of $10,000 as a dowry to give the couple a good start and to cover the birth of their first child.

Rivka was described as a quiet person who came from a family of prosperous Israeli settlers who had lived in Safed, considered one of Judaism's Four Holy Cities since the 16th century as well as a center of kabbalistic study. I believe Rivka's bloodline traced back directly to King David, which meant her family was connected to every prominent rabbi throughout history, including the revered Baal Shem Tov. Rivka's father was a fourth or fifth generation Israeli whose ancestors were buried in the ancient Old Jewish Cemetery, near where the great Kabbalist Rav Isaac Luria (the Ari) had been entombed centuries earlier. Since the Rav's ancestors were not particularly distinguished, this union to Rivka was a source of great pride for his parents.

The Rav moved with his new bride to a three-story duplex in a Jewish neighborhood near Eastern Parkway and Prospect Park in Brooklyn, where many Orthodox Chassidic Jews still live today. There they began a family that eventually grew to include eight children—four boys and four girls. With his dowry, the Rav acquired the row house with its coffered ceilings, and he and his family lived upstairs while they rented the ground level to a store and the second floor to another family. They lived four blocks from Rivka's sister, who made her home on Carroll Street. Although her parents still lived in Israel, Rivka's brother was nearby as well. The Rav's parents now lived in the beach community of Rockaway, and his brother Sigmund was in the Flatbush section of Brooklyn.

Although he gave every appearance of having settled into the traditional life of a rabbi, after a few years of teaching young children, the Rav's soul began to stir. Soon it became apparent that this work didn't suit him. He was restless. He kept asking himself, "How much can I really accomplish here?" He was also becoming disillusioned by Orthodox Judaism as it had been taught to him. He felt that it didn't provide enough practical solutions to life's real problems. He needed to try his hand at something else.

It's important to keep in mind that even though my husband was disenchanted, he never left the fold of Jewish Orthodoxy. Nor did he ever really stop being an educator. After all, the Rav was a Leo, and they are born teachers.

Philip Gruberger went into business with his brother-in-law, Herschel Wuilliger, Rivka's sister's husband. Shraga Feivel was my husband's Hebrew name. Phillip was the English equivalent of Feivel and it was the name he used in more public settings. Gruberger was shortened to Berg later when we moved to Israel. Philip Gruberger and Herschel Wullinger became insurance agents and opened an office in downtown Brooklyn, on 127 Remsen Street, close to Borough Hall. Here they wrote insurance policies for government and city buildings in New York. They also insured general contractors.

It's customary for Orthodox men and married women to cover their heads at all times. A man wears a hat or *kippah* (skullcap) while a woman wears a wig or hat. The Rav would never meet anyone with his head uncovered, yet in certain business situations he felt he could not wear a *kippah* or hat so he would wear a toupee, the "rug" on his head took care of this problem.

They quickly prospered. Given that so many of his clients were involved in government, the Rav developed warm relationships with many politicians in the late 1950s and early 60s. This allowed him to serve as a connector between the religious and secular worlds, a role he would continue to play throughout his life. Prior to his involvement, Orthodox Jews in New York had been quite insular and had little political impact. But the Rav began to change this dynamic. He was the first person to bring people like New York Mayor Robert Wagner to visit with the leaders of various Orthodox and ultra-Orthodox communities.

He was only in his early thirties when he introduced government power brokers to the Chassidic community, his friends, and neighbors, in the hopes that both groups would better understand each other. He became an advisor to Councilman Paul R. Screvane, President of the New York City Council, accepting only one dollar a year for his services. Once a city garbage truck driver, Screvane had become a powerful figure in New York's Democratic politics. Screvane served as campaign manager for both of Robert Wagner's mayoral campaigns, and for Robert F. Kennedy's Senate campaign. He organized the city's role in President Lyndon B. Johnson's war on poverty, and worked with Robert Moses to mount the 1964 World's Fair. His close ties to Screvane made the Rav a player. As Yisrael Lifschultz, a reporter for *Jewish Look New York* put it in 1975, this young, "enterprising rabbi jumped the political fence with the grace and agility of an Olympic hurdler."

* * *

In 1958, I was sixteen and living with my grandma Rose. I'd been tossed around quite a bit as a child, and I needed to support myself to finish high school. I'd taken an afterschool job at a Regency insurance agency in Brooklyn, where I worked for six months as a private assistant. I answered phones, greeted clients, made appointments, and opened mail. My employers, Rabbi Philip Gruberger and Hershel Wuilliger, were subletting their modest offices from a much larger insurance agent. I thought it pretty clever that when our clients came in for meetings they walked past a sea of desks to the space where the Regency office was located. It conveyed the impression that these were all Gruberger and Wuillliger employees, and that the business was much more successful than it actually was in those early days.

The Rav spent most of his time in the field—meeting clients, looking for business, and evaluating contractors for policies. Hershel anchored the office, so I spent more time working with him. In retrospect, it's clear that Rabbi Philip Gruberger was oblivious to me at that time. Spark? There was nothing between us.

First of all, he was much older than me—I was just a kid. But I also didn't particularly like him. He was a powerful businessman with a deeply religious upbringing, and I was a brash, non-observant, rebellious teenage girl. We had nothing in common. During that time, the Rav and I were like pork and cheese—complete opposites—prohibited by Jewish law from being served at the same table!

I remember one of the few instances when my boss took any notice of me. Late one afternoon, as I was about to leave the office, one of our phones rang. It was an inside line, a number that most people didn't have. The man on the other end inquired, "Can I speak to Rabbi Gruberger?"

I asked, "Who's calling, please?"

"This is Mayor Wagner," he said, to which I retorted, "Yes, and I'm the Pope." Assuming it was a prank call, I hung up!

Rabbi Gruberger came over and asked, "What was that all about?"

"Oh," I said off-handedly, "some man called claiming he was Mayor Wagner."

Rabbi Gruberger turned white with anger. "That was the Mayor!" he yelled at me. "Get him on the line, now!" And I quickly back-pedaled to fix my mistake.

The Rav's influence on behalf of his community was far reaching in those days. For instance, in New York City there are strict regulations about alternate side of the street parking. When these rules are in effect (which is most weekdays), people can't park on one side of the street or the other, and their cars are ticketed or towed if they don't comply. Although this allows the city's street sweepers to do their work, it reduces the number of available parking spaces by nearly half on any given day.

The city suspended these rules for certain holidays like Thanksgiving, Christmas, and New Year's Day, and as needed for blizzards or other emergencies. However, they posed a special hardship for observant Jews, especially when major holidays such as Rosh Hashanah and Yom Kippur fell on weekdays. Since Orthodox Jews don't drive on those days they couldn't move their cars. Exercising his clout with the Mayor's office, the Rav was able to see to it that these parking rules were suspended during important Jewish Holy Days as well.

He also helped to change the Blue Laws in New York City. These laws, instituted by Puritans in Connecticut before the American Revolution, prohibited stores and other businesses from opening on Sundays. However, they created an unfair burden for observant Jewish merchants, since they were also obligated to close up shop on Saturdays for Shabbat. Going dark on both weekend days meant Jewish storekeepers lost a lot of business.

Although Blue Laws have long since been abolished in New York, the Rav helped make them more flexible. Owners could be open for business on Saturdays or on Sundays, but not both. Jewish shopkeepers were no longer at a competitive disadvantage. Working people from throughout the city soon flocked to the open shops in Jewish neighborhoods to make their purchases on Sundays, when all the other stores in the city were shuttered. In these and other ways, the Rav made it possible for his community to prosper.

Over the next few years, Philip Gruberger became wealthy, expanding his insurance agency's reach to include contractors working on large housing projects in high-rise buildings in Coney Island and the Bensonhurst section of Brooklyn. As he became familiar with the ins and outs of local real estate, the Rav began leveraging income from the insurance business to invest in apartment buildings in

Brooklyn and Queens. He managed these himself, without his partner.

For most people this would have been impossible, given that he was already working long hours in the insurance business. But my husband wasn't most people. He had a huge capacity for work—nothing was ever too much for him. There was no limit to his vision moving forward. He was also never satisfied, but in a good way. No matter what he achieved—and this would later apply to the dissemination of kabbalistic wisdom—he always knew that more was possible.

Yes, Philip Gruberger became a millionaire, although even then his goal was not just to create wealth. He had a strong need to share his resources where he felt they would make a difference, donating to political figures and religious causes and schools. At one point, when his alma mater, Beth Medrash Govoha in Lakewood, New Jersey, needed a new building, he organized a big fundraising dinner, giving a large donation himself, and collecting money from others. In its gratitude, the school engraved his name on the plaque of donors posted prominently on the building wall.

As a sign of his growing wealth and political influence in the early 1960s, Philip Gruberger was invited by his friend, Teddy Kennedy, to spend time at the family compound in Hyannisport. He also attended John F. Kennedy's birthday party in New York and was welcomed at the White House, where for a few moments he found himself exchanging private pleasantries with the President. In fact, he had the honor of being the first person ever to be served a kosher meal in the White House.

A highly respected, trusted, and successful member of his community, young Philip Gruberger forged ahead in the trajectory one might expect from a man with his energy, connections, and business acumen. But then, in 1962, the Rav's beloved mother, Esther Gruberger, died.

And everything changed.

CHAPTER 2:

SOUL MATES: MEETING RAV BRANDWEIN

According to Kabbalah every soul has two halves, which means that each and every one of us has a counterpart in this world—the other half of our soul, or soul mate. The Zohar, the foundational text of Kabbalah, describes a soul mate as the perfect match established for each human being at the time of the creation of the world. Soul mates find each other across great distances and even through many lifetimes. Like all of our important relationships, this one is directed by a process called *tikkun*, the mending of the soul that is our work in this lifetime.

A kabbalistic soul mate bond includes more than just two entities. It's the merging of two individuals with a third partner, the Light of the Creator. Mutual desire for the Light is the glue of this connection. These relationships can be romantic, however, they can also include parent and child, as well as teacher and student. What's important is that such unions consist of two people who have joined forces to connect with the Light to advance spiritual understanding, to make the world better through their bond.

Sometimes there is conflict in these matches, and the soul mate aspect may not be apparent to the world, or even to the individuals themselves. But this doesn't affect the significance of the bond.

I believe that the Rav's teacher, Rav Yehuda Tzvi Brandwein, was his soul mate. They found each other halfway around the world and united to reveal the Light and advance spiritual understanding. At times, there was dissension surrounding their relationship but peace within, which is a quality typical of soul mates. In letters the Rav received from his teacher during the seven years they studied together beginning in 1962, Rav Brandwein referred to my husband as *Yedid Nafshi*, which translates to "Beloved of My Soul." The Light kept them together. And, as you'll see, this connection was so intense that the Rav longed to be with his teacher night and day.

The Rav changed because of what his teacher meant to him. Many recognized Rav Brandwein's unique qualities, and my husband felt them so deeply that once they'd met, he was able to do or think of little else. As the Rav once put it in an interview, "My whole way of life and world outlook was totally transformed" as a result of this seemingly chance meeting.

How did all this occur? After his mother Esther's passing in 1962, the Rav and his family decided she should be buried in Jerusalem, so he traveled to Israel with his mother's body for the funeral. Among those who came to pay a *shiva* (condolence) call following the burial was his wife's uncle, Rivka's father's brother—Rav Yehuda Tzvi Brandwein.

At first glance, Rav Brandwein looked like a typical ultra-Orthodox Jew. He dressed in a black hat and robe and wore *peyois* (sidelocks). He had a long mustache and patchy beard that looked as if he never shaved it, as was the custom. He was shorter than my husband, maybe 5'8", and walked with the help of a cane. He had sizeable workman's hands, having toiled as a bricklayer in the 1930s, but now they were soft, and his eyes were large and wise, as if he'd witnessed a great deal in his lifetime. He exuded kindness with all his being, and my bereaved husband was immediately drawn to him.

Although this was the first time they had met in person, Yehuda Tzvi Brandwein was no stranger to Philip Gruberger. He had heard about Rav Brandwein during family gatherings and discussions but none of the conversation had registered deeply because it wasn't yet time for them to connect. He was aware, however, that his wife's family felt some animosity toward Rav Brandwein. They didn't support his study of Kabbalah or his decision to become Head Rabbi of the anti-religious Histadrut, which we'll explore in an upcoming chapter. Philip Gruberger knew that Rav Brandwein was considered somewhat of a rebel, and believed that Rivka's family worried that his commitment to Kabbalah might reflect poorly on them.

Indeed, most of the Orthodox and ultra-Orthodox communities around the world at that time frowned upon the study of Kabbalah. As a powerful and well-to-do family, the Brandweins were able to exert their influence to thwart Rav Brandwein's involvement. The story goes that they owned a Jerusalem bus line, for example, and ordered the drivers not to pick up Rav Brandwein as he made his way to study with his teacher, Rav Yehuda Leib HaLevi Ashlag, on the outskirts of the city.

So Rav Brandwein walked for hours in the dark so he could study with his teacher after midnight—that time of the day when kabbalists believe we are closest to the Light. Together they studied and discussed Kabbalah until dawn. This journey was dangerous because in the days before Israel gained statehood, Jordanian snipers targeted travelers on the road. In fact, one of the British police commanders who governed Palestine at that time cited Rav Brandwein as an example of bravery to his own officers. Upon hearing this story later, the Rav took it as evidence of his teacher's unshakable commitment.

The Rav was aware of Kabbalah, of course, but since it fell outside of a traditional Orthodox education he had never explored it. At the time, Kabbalah was studied privately, as it had been for millennia. This mystical, secretly encoded form of Judaism could only be approached by married Jewish men over forty who were already deeply steeped in the Torah and could find a teacher to guide them in their pursuit of this esoteric study. Many believed that a man who was unprepared would go mad if he attempted to learn the sacred wisdom and teachings of Kabbalah, and it was completely off limits for women and non-Jews.

By the time Philip Gruberger arrived in Israel at age thirty-five for his mother's funeral, he was looking for a respite from the rough-and-tumble New York business and political arena in which he had prospered. His life as a wealthy businessman had neither satisfied his hunger for spirituality nor eased his disillusionment with Orthodoxy. Still a young man at thirty-five, he described his state of mind this way. "I was an observant Jew who, being so completely consumed by the materialistic world, carried out the *mitzvot* (precepts) and the study of Divine Law in a perfunctory manner, without delving into the reasons for doing these things. As a result of this unquestioning attitude, I was truly at a loss to explain why I went through the motions of performing the precepts."

He was primed for a spiritual awakening.

* * *

My husband would always describe the moment he met Rav Brandwein as a pivotal event in his life. Before that time, Kabbalah was as foreign to Philip Gruberger as the surface of the moon. Since the Orthodox tradition frowned on the study of Kabbalah, he had steered clear of this dangerous subject. But all this was about to change.

When Rav Brandwein's hand touched his in a handshake, my husband experienced a jolt of energy, an outpouring of Light running from this gentle rabbi directly into Philip Gruberger's body. He described himself as "just melting away.... It was like he was comforting my soul in his wonderful warm hands. It was indeed an amazing feeling. I had no explanation of that most memorable first encounter."

In that instant, Rabbi Philip Gruberger understood that Rav Brandwein would be his teacher, and that his life would never be the same. The man he had known himself to be dissolved; everything that had defined him disappeared in that moment as he stepped into an alternate universe. Rabbi Philip Gruberger left this plane, and in his place, the seed of the person who would become Rav Berg began to incubate.

How is this possible? Kabbalists believe that a veil exists between the physical world and the upper, spiritual realms of existence. But once in a while, punctures in the veil allow rays of the Light to shine through. These allow us to receive messages from the Creator that help us fulfill our destiny, "Aha!" moments that tell us, "From now on, your existence will not be the same." This is what's known as *Bat Kol*, a Divine voice or call.

To sense these messages from the Creator, messages that ask us to give our souls the chance to fulfill their destiny, we have to be open to them. Sadly, we're usually too distracted, so we deflect or ignore them. This leaves us with a yearning, an emptiness inside, and we don't know why. But in the moment Rabbi Philip Gruberger touched his teacher's hand, he had a flash of insight. He knew he was being called to leave behind the life he had known.

My husband never felt like a victim, despite all the hardships to follow. He never once said, "Oh my God, I came to Israel, I met my teacher, and then my whole life started falling apart." Instead he embraced this change fully and whole-heartedly. That moment he touched his teacher was accompanied by Light and awe. My husband had found his soul mate; suddenly he was awakened to his soul's destiny, with all of its gifts and challenges.

I, for one, am sure that this was not the first time Philip Gruberger had arrived on this plane to engage in the study of Kabbalah. Who knows how often his soul and that of Rav Brandwein had connected in earlier lifetimes? Who knows how many times they had been united as master and student?

I like to think of their brief meeting in 1962 as a door suddenly opening onto a path illuminated by Light from the souls of great kabbalists past. We normally understand the word "lineage" as being tied to physical offspring and DNA. But spiritual lineage is often identified in different terms; it's associated with one soul entering and uplifting another. This means that the sparks of the souls of sages in history often enter mystics of future generations. That's how the latter gain wisdom and strength to do what their souls came into this lifetime to achieve.

I have no way of knowing for certain whether my husband was the reincarnation of an earlier kabbalist, but I do know that he succeeded in bringing about the next significant revelation of this wisdom, and by so doing became part of that lineage. Consider for a moment the great sages that came before my husband.

Four thousand years ago, Abraham realized that there is an unseen Divine force, or energy, if you will, which exists both outside of and within all things. And on this hidden level of reality the entire universe interconnects to form a unified whole. Abraham's purpose was to make all of mankind aware of this hidden truth. This was his life's work. To this end, the patriarch created the *Sefer Yetzirah* ("Book of Formation"), which sets forth the glory of God's universe in one encoded document.

Remarkably, this wisdom was compressed into only a few pages, much like Einstein's formula $E=MC^2$. Abraham's work contains all of the spiritual equations concerning our world of time, space, and motion—all the secrets of existence—from the Creation of the world to the various paradigms that we experience through our senses as reality. It would take millennia to unravel the spiritual energy locked inside his Book of Formation.

Two thousand years later, when the Romans ruled the land of Israel, the Zohar emerged through the work of Rav Shimon Bar Yochai. His teacher, Rabbi Akiva, was considered preeminent among sages for his contributions to the Mishnah and other learned Jewish writings. During the Bar Kochba Revolt around 132–136 CE, a decree by the Roman Emperor forbade Talmudic studies. When Rabbi Akiva refused to obey their order, the Romans sentenced him to death for continuing to teach the Torah and its secrets.

More than a half million Jews died in that revolt, including 24,000 of Rabbi Akiva's students, and thousands more perished from hunger and disease, or were taken captive and sold into slavery. Before he was executed, Rabbi Akiva passed on the precepts of Kabbalah to his disciple, Rav Shimon. Fearing for his life, Rav Shimon sought refuge with his son in a cave in Peki'in, Israel and remained there for thirteen years. During this long isolation, he received instruction in Kabbalah from Moses and Elijah, who visited him in visions. This is how the Zohar, the Book of Splendor, was revealed.

When a new Roman emperor came into power, Rav Shimon and his son felt safe enough to return to Jerusalem and Safed. As laid out by Rabbi Akiva, their job with the teachings they had been given was to "reveal and conceal them at the same time." First, to make sure the mystical secrets of the universe were not lost to future generations, Rav Shimon called upon his student, Rav Aba, to record this wisdom. Rav Aba had an extraordinary gift for the abstract language of metaphor and parable. Now the kabbalistic secrets were safe, deftly concealed inside stories that made it difficult for the unworthy to grasp and misuse this ancient power.

The Zohar expounded on concepts that were centuries ahead of their time. In an age when everyone believed that the world was flat, the Zohar depicted our planet as spherical, with people experiencing day and night at the same time but in different time zones. The Zohar described the moment of Creation as a Big Bang-like explosion. It explored the notion of parallel universes. Yet as expressed by Rav Shimon, the Zohar was much more than a book of spiritual wisdom. Its very words and pages contained a powerful energy; it was a tool imbued with the *Or haGanuz* (Hidden Light).

Our job is to reveal that Light of the Creator, and by doing so to bring about fulfillment, peace, protection, healing, and the ultimate removal of chaos. Rav Shimon foresaw a day when the spiritual wisdom of Kabbalah would be available to everyone. But until that day came, the original manuscripts of the Zohar would have to remain concealed. He anticipated that these ideas would be considered frightening and heretical. So they were hidden away for centuries. And Western society plunged into the Dark Ages.

The secrets of the Zohar were lost for the next 1,200 years. Then they resurfaced in Spain as a collection of essays during the thirteenth century. Rabbi Moses de León is believed to be the person who rediscovered the Zohar, but no one knows exactly how that happened. Some people believe he bought the ancient writing from Crusaders returning to Europe from Spain. Others say that the King of Spain had them in his possession. However it came to pass, from that moment on, the Zohar was disseminated more widely. Centers of study arose, and although this material was still closely held, it broadly influenced Jewish ethics, prayer, customs, Shabbat, and holiday rituals.

Several centuries passed. In 1556, at the age of 22, Rav Isaac Luria, known as the Ari or Holy Lion, began to study and interpret the Zohar. A venerated mystic and kabbalist, he lived in Jerusalem and Safed along with many other rabbis and holy men who had escaped the Spanish Inquisition. By the time he left this plane at the age of 38, he had decoded the Zohar and authored a set of writings based on it that lays out layers of hidden spiritual meaning in the Torah and the *mitzvot*—delineating the *kavanot* (spiritual intention) and practice that we use today.

The Ari wrote about reincarnation and Divine Inspiration, and he described the physical and spiritual reality that governs the universe in terms of ten levels of energy or Sefirot. These begin at the lowest rung with the material world that we humans inhabit (Malchut is the dimension known as the "Kingdom") and reach to the uppermost level—Keter, the crown. His writings describe that although every soul is given the opportunity to climb this ladder, this spiritual journey involves setbacks and may take place over many lifetimes.

The Ari lived as a hermit for thirteen years while he probed the Zohar's mysteries. He was said to have meditated on single verses for months at a time until their hidden meanings were revealed to him. He uncovered extraordinary secrets inside the Zohar's poetic words. The Ari's greatest legacy is the *Kitvei ha Ari* ("Writings of the Ari"), compiled by his cherished student, Rav Chaim Vital. This profound work gave birth to Lurianic Kabbalah, the definitive school of kabbalistic thought.

Jewish and Christian scholars alike were drawn to the Ari's writings and the Zohar, believing they held the keys to understanding our world. These works had a dramatic impact on intellectual pursuits during the late Renaissance, profoundly influencing Sir Isaac Newton and

Gottfried Wilhelm von Leibniz, the German philosopher and mathematician who invented calculus. During this period of intellectual ferment, when the separate domains of science, philosophy, and spirituality were merging, Kabbalist Rav Abraham Azulai inferred that from the year 1540 and onward, the basic levels of Kabbalah must be taught publicly to everyone, young and old. Only through Kabbalah will we forever eliminate war, destruction, and man's inhumanity to his fellow man.

This only came to pass in our own lifetime, with the help of Kabbalah Centres around the world. The Ari laid the essential groundwork translating and decoding these manuscripts. He took a compressed document that was nearly opaque and turned it into writings from which scholars could learn and teach. The Rav, his teacher Rav Brandwein, and his teacher before him Rav Yehuda Ashlag, made this wisdom increasingly available. Their goal was to bring the Ari's sparks to the world, by creating a system people could use to apply Kabbalah to their daily lives. Of course, all of that would come many centuries later; and there were still great obstacles to contend with.

One was posed by a 17th century Jewish mystic, Shabbatai Tzvi. He studied kabbalistic writings for years but twisted their deepest meanings for his own benefit and eventually declared himself the Messiah. Supported by his many followers, he created chaos and dissension within the Jewish world, only to be excommunicated from Judaism and imprisoned in Turkey. There, he converted to Islam to save his own life—a shock that continues to reverberate throughout the Jewish Orthodox community. The Rav described Shabbatai Tzvi's legacy this way: "There is the fear that the study of Kabbalah will lead one to become a heretic." It's little wonder that Rav Brandwein's family opposed his kabbalistic endeavors.

The Shabbatai Tzvi fiasco tainted the study of Kabbalah. In the minds of most rabbis the wisdom contained in the Zohar became something dangerous, and its study was relegated to a shadowy world. During the Age of Enlightenment, eighteenth century rabbis prohibited unsupervised access to the writings. Even when printing presses made books more readily available, many rabbis sought to transmit the manuscripts in handwritten form to strictly limit their distribution. Some of the wisdom was encoded so that only those previously trained in Kabbalah could read it.

However, this knowledge and the Light it conveys was difficult to suppress, and it began to emerge in other ways. By the 1800s, a class system had developed among Jews: the wealthy and more educated looked down upon the majority, many of whom couldn't read Hebrew or recite the prayers. However, in the Ukraine there arose a great new rabbi, Israel Ben Eliezer, known as the Baal Shem Tov, who began a spiritual revolution. Although few people spoke of the Zohar or the writings of the Ari, the Baal Shem Tov's revolution drew directly from these sources. His basic tenets were love for one another and spiritual democracy.

The Baal Shem Tov brought mysticism to the masses by focusing on a majority of Jews, giving them importance and elevating them spiritually. People being so poor and life so difficult, he taught through storytelling and acts of kindness. He met the people where they were. He taught that sometimes the simplest person's prayer is more powerful than the greatest sage. He reinvigorated the spirituality in Judaism and founded the Chassidic movement with the mystical themes of the Ari running like a vein of gold through his tales and parables. It is a tremendous gift to be able to speak to someone without formal training on Kabbalah and still make the subject understandable—a gift that the Rav would eventually share.

In the early 20th century, Rav Yehuda Ashlag, who would become Rav Brandwein's teacher, took his place in a line of brilliant scholars with the tenacity to hold firm to their soul's purpose, no matter the obstacle. Born in 1885, Rav Ashlag melded the teachings of the Zohar with the masters who came before him—the Ari and the Baal Shem Tov—creating brilliant new ways of explaining Kabbalah. Up until Rav Ashlag's involvement, only a select few understood the Zohar itself, printed as it was in Aramaic and published in a three-volume set.

Rav Ashlag wrote the first complete Modern Hebrew translation and commentary on the Zohar, as well as a series of essays that organized and explained in depth the teachings of the Ari—a pinnacle in Kabbalah history because it marked the first time these writings had been made available to the layperson. He called his work *HaSulam* ("The Ladder")—a step-by-step guide people could use to ascend to the highest levels of spirituality. Rav Ashlag believed that the precept "Love Your Neighbor as Yourself" would serve as the foundation of the future world.

This holy man established the very first Kabbalah Centre, Beit Ulpana, in the city of Jerusalem where, as tradition dictated, he made Kabbalah available to men over the age of forty who were already steeped in their religious studies. Although many leading rabbis of his generation applauded this historic event, others vehemently opposed it, calling him a sinner and a heretic, fanning the controversy around disseminating this spiritual wisdom. Passions ran so high that Rav Ashlag was beaten on the steps outside his synagogue and left lying in his own blood.

Rav Ashlag's writings describe ways to address the chaos that has plagued humankind since time immemorial, and touch on topics like relativity, space travel, medical science, and other matters affecting the welfare of humanity first concealed in the Zohar, 2,000 years earlier. Rav Ashlag's genius lay in his ability to extrapolate these secrets from the Ari's 500-year-old writings. As these mysteries were unveiled they were injected into the collective unconscious, influencing his counterparts toiling in the world of physics. On the unseen spiritual level, his work ignited the technological explosion of the 20th century.

Rav Ashlag wrote that at different moments in human history, unique means were needed to reach people. Using the example of a person drowning in the ocean, he said, "If you see his hand, you try to grab his hand. If you see his head, you try to grab his hair to save him." The Baal Shem Tov had tried to save people through their souls; his teachings were directed toward the heart. During the time of the Ari, the way to save souls was through the mind, so many of his teachings are didactic, detailed, and deeply intellectual. Rav Ashlag believed that today's world needs both, so he acted as a funnel merging the spiritual streams that came before him to create a new way. His teachings contained two elements: ideas from past masters, translated and explained, and new revelations from the Creator for our generation. He often wrote that the wisdom came through him. This was not due to his great merit but because of our generation's need for this revelation.

Rav Ashlag had a strong personality. One of his students once asked him "When I go to the *mikvah*, what should I think about?" The *mikvah* is a purification bath used for spiritual immersion. Rav Ashlag replied to his student, "Meditate that any blockages stopping the Light of the Creator from being revealed should be blown up and sent away." Pleased by this advice, the student started to leave for the *mikvah* when Rav Ashlag called him back. "You should also meditate that if you're the blockage for the Light of the Creator, you should be sent away as well."

Each great kabbalist was responsible for a certain revelation of Light that contained the sparks of the souls of those who came before him. Every generation gave rise to another level of understanding. Like the peeling of an onion, another layer was removed, another veil taken down, exposing this universal wisdom that was, is, and always will be available for more and more people to see. Rabbi Akiva possessed the courage to sacrifice his own life to continue the teaching of the Torah. Rav Shimon decoded the Torah by revealing the Zohar. The Ari explained the Zohar. The Baal Shem Tov turned the work of the Ari into action. Rav Ashlag explained the Ari and translated the Zohar into Modern Hebrew. Rav Brandwein clarified Rav Ashlag. Each made a contribution that was expanded on by the one who followed.

When you look at the history of great kabbalists, you'll see that my husband exemplified many qualities of the legendary teachers who had gone before him. His soul contained Rabbi Akiva's fearlessness, Rav Shimon's certainty that the Zohar would bring the redemption of the world, the Ari's brilliance, the Baal Shem Tov's accessibility, Rav Ashlag's tenacity, and Rav Brandwein' heart. These attributes allowed him to achieve what no one had ever accomplished before: fully open up Kabbalah to the world.

In one seemingly innocuous moment, when he shook hands with Rav Brandwein at a funeral, my husband connected to all the great kabbalists throughout history. By doing so, he committed himself to taking the next bold step in disseminating the wisdom of Kabbalah. For Rav Ashlag, and even for Rav Brandwein, the idea of distributing millions of Zohars around the world was not even within the realm of possibility. And yet, just a few decades later, the Rav would make this a reality.

Fifty years ago, before the Kabbalah Centre came into being, if you wanted to study the Zohar you would have had to find a master somewhere. If you were lucky enough to succeed in doing so, you probably would not have had access to the Zohar. All the money in the world wouldn't buy you a copy of your own. But today, millions of people own and study the Zohar. This was the fruit of the Rav's soul work. And it all began the moment he touched Rav Brandwein's hand.

Before his death, Rav Ashlag told Rav Brandwein that he would soon merit his own students, and that one of them would help bring this wisdom to the world amid great protest and scorn. Had he envisioned the arrival of Philip Gruberger—next in a long line of kabbalists stretching back more than 2,000 years?

Philip Gruberger paid Rav Brandwein's wife to sleep somewhere else so he could study and learn with his teacher at midnight—that auspicious time to explore spiritual texts. This is how much he loved the man and yearned to be in his presence. This was not a physical love but a profoundly spiritual one that I liken to the devotion between King David and Jonathan. Theirs was so great that Jonathan relinquished his kingdom to save David's life. There are those who misunderstand and misrepresent that spiritual bond also. My husband's relationship with his teacher reminds me of the story of Abraham. Once the Patriarch understood that there was one Creator of all things, all he could think about was coming to know and connect with the Creator. When you love that much, you cannot bear to be apart from your beloved.

Let's be clear, though. All this didn't just happen to him. My husband *chose* to take on a new future. It was a choice that changed the world. In fact, I often wonder how different things would be if these two men had merely shaken hands and gone their separate ways, if the Rav had ignored the divine call and returned instead to New York to pick up his life where he'd left off. Fortunately, he had an amazing capacity to embrace opportunity. The Rav's destiny directed him down a new path; it was the openness already within him that allowed him to explore, discover, and embrace ways to make people's lives better.

We must keep in mind that by contrast, the Orthodox society from which Philip Gruberger had emerged was small, rigid, and exclusive. For the first thirty-five years of his life he adhered to his community's expectations, including everything his parents wanted: he married a woman with an important rabbinical lineage, he carefully followed all of the rules, and he became first a teacher and then a successful businessman. He never deviated from the prescribed path. But the moment he and Rav Brandwein touched, he was cast free from his limiting reality. Suddenly everything was different. Rav Brandwein's light penetrated Philip Gruberger's being and awakened it. In that one instant, he let go of his upbringing with its conventional limitations and began to embrace an alternate way of being.

I often think of the courage this required of him—the willingness to let go of everything that felt familiar with no knowledge of what was to come. My husband would say, "I would have taken a bullet for my teacher," and in a way he did. The changes he made in his life were tantamount to death—and eventually to rebirth.

The Rav once said that our judgments govern our influence over the environment. How many of us can point to anything significant in our lives that varies much from what our parents, children, other relatives, teachers, clergy, and employers have determined to be proper behavior? Yet until we leave comfort and familiarity behind and accept that we determine our own experience, everything we know will remain the same.

This is the way of things from generation to generation. Dates and locations change, but we yield to the gravitational pull of the familiar. Very few of us ask, "How can I change the world?" Philip Gruberger did. Once he connected with Rav Brandwein, the Rav single-mindedly pursued a goal on behalf of all humankind: dispelling the illusion that we are separate by revealing the truth that we are one.

The Rav would dismiss the notion that he was somehow special by saying, "The Kabbalah Centre is a thought in the Creator's mind, and the Rav is a thought in the Creator's mind. If it wasn't Philip Berg, it would be someone else." By this he meant that the task of leading the effort to disseminate kabbalistic wisdom was what actually mattered. He just happened to be filling that job at the moment but tomorrow it would be another person. His ego was not involved, although he never for a moment took for granted his good fortune in being able to take on this role.

In the presence of a true kabbalist, Philip Gruberger was transformed, his consciousness awakened. Yet despite his intensive Jewish education, Kabbalah still remained a shadowy and mysterious subject. "Why shouldn't I learn about it?" he thought. He had always been inquisitive, especially within the confines of Judaism. Besides, something had stirred deep inside that he had never felt before and could not deny. Many had interacted with Rav Brandwein but in him, my husband had found his teacher.

When the two men began to talk at the funeral, Rav Brandwein asked Philip Gruberger, "Would you support my Yeshiva?"

The Rav eagerly replied, "Yes, I will, if you teach me Kabbalah." Although he knew next to nothing about Rav Brandwein's life, he was drawn to this gentle, soft-spoken man by a force he couldn't explain. Without knowing what it would lead to, he felt lucky when Rav Brandwein agreed to this arrangement. It felt right.

To immerse himself in study with Rav Brandwein, Philip Gruberger took extended leaves of absence from his businesses. This meant leaving behind his family, his insurance company, and his real estate holdings for months on end to be at his teacher's side. Rav Brandwein taught in a donated building in the Old City of Jerusalem. Originally called Beit Ulpana, a school established by Rav Ashlag in 1922, now it was Rav Brandwein's Yeshiva Kol Yehuda, the institution the Rav had promised to support. The two men also met at Rav Brandwein's home in Tel Aviv near the old Shuk, an outdoor market. When in Tel Aviv, my husband lived in the suburb of Kiryat Ono. Like his teacher before him, he often walked many miles to study with his master, doing so unfailingly on Shabbat.

Since Philip Gruberger's conversational Hebrew was poor and Rav Brandwein couldn't speak English, they communicated in Yiddish, the language of European Jewry. Rav Brandwein also taught three or four other men—considered the proper size group to learn Kabbalah at the time—including his son and son-in-law. They did this discreetly, since this study would not have been tolerated in their community. My husband now took his place in this small, clandestine group.

* * *

The primary focus of Kabbalah has been acquiring the concealed knowledge of the Creator, including the Creator's designs for the seen and the unseen universe. The Rav said that Kabbalah offers more insight into this knowledge than any other wisdom or tradition because it is the source of these other traditions. This is written in the Zohar's interpretation of the verse in Genesis 25:6: "And unto the sons of the concubines that Abraham had, Abraham gave them gifts... and sent them unto the east country." "The 'east country' refers to places such as India," the Rav explained, "while the gifts alluded to certain spiritual teachings, but not *all* of the teachings. The complete system of spirituality, however, was passed by Abraham to his son Isaac for future generations."

Rav Brandwein's small study group, which now embraced my husband, explored this knowledge concealed within the Zohar along with a huge array of essays and explications written by the Ari and Rav Yehuda Ashlag. These included Rav Ashlag's work *Talmud Eser Sefirot* ("Study of the Ten Luminous Emanations") that explains the ten levels of energy set forth by the Ari. My husband found the long hours of *limudim*—learning together—deeply satisfying. He described feeling drawn to this great wisdom as if by a powerful magnet. In the pages he pored over late at night, Philip Gruberger finally found the inner meaning he'd been searching for all his life. He carried a volume of the *Talmud Eser Sefiro*t with him everywhere, reading and rereading every passage, and each time it provided new insights. In fact, he would never finish reading it, since the text evolves alongside the reader's consciousness throughout a lifetime.

As his studies continued over the next several years, my husband began editing, translating, and publishing additional books with Rav Brandwein. The Ari's writings, for instance, hadn't been organized in a coherent way up until this point. My husband and Rav Brandwein sorted and arranged these works and then published them in fourteen volumes. They also worked with Rav Ashlag's material, publishing a ten-volume edition of *HaSulam* ("The Ladder"), Rav Ashlag's extensive commentary on the Zohar. They translated other portions of the Zohar accompanied by Rav Brandwein's commentaries such as the Tikunei Zohar, which was revealed to Rav Shimon, his son, and eight disciples in the Idra Raba) and *Hashmotot haZohar* ("Addendum of the Zohar," of Rav Shimon Bar Yochai). In 1965, my husband established the religious organization, National Institute for Research in Kabbalah. He located it in New York, so he could begin distributing some of these books in the U.S.

I once stood with the Rav and our sons at the graves of Rav Ashlag and Rav Brandwein, who are buried side by side in the Har HaMenuchot Cemetery in Jerusalem. The Rav began talking to the spirits of his teachers. "You have to help me in all the work I am doing," he said to them. "You have to help me. Do you know why? Because I am your servant." The Rav believed with every fiber of his being—as I do—that the highest attainment of this lifetime is service to those who teach us, to act on behalf of the Light of the Creator. And from the moment he met Rav Brandwein, my husband was on his way.

CHAPTER 3:

LEARNING FROM RAV YEHUDA TZVI BRANDWEIN: THE ACTIVIST KABBALIST

The study and publication of kabbalistic texts were only the beginning of my husband's education. He learned at least as much from the many real world observations, experiences, and interactions he had with his teacher. In fact, those exchanges were what transformed him most profoundly and taught him a different way of being.

When Philip Gruberger returned to Israel to study with his teacher for the first time and fully immerse himself in Kabbalah, he expected that Rav Brandwein would push aside everything else and focus only on teaching him. He imagined he would sit with his master and that they would study together night and day. But instead of plunging into an exploration of the Zohar that first meeting, when Rav Brandwein saw his new student he said, "You're here! Great! Start packing these boxes of books. We need to send them out today."

My husband was stunned. "Me? Pack books? I didn't come here for that! I came to learn with you. I can pay for someone else to pack books. You're supposed to be my teacher." A young Leo who had already achieved wealth and political influence, the Rav couldn't understand why he'd be assigned such a menial task. It felt demeaning, especially since he had just flown to Israel from New York to begin his studies.

But Rav Brandwein was undeterred. "Listen," he told my husband in his firm, gentle way, "you are going to pack the books with me first. Then you'll go with me to the post office, and we're going to send them out. We will reveal far more Light this way than we would through study. If you and I study a few hours now, we can make some progress but if we pack these books then 100 people could begin studying. Imagine all that additional Light in the world."

Rabbi Gruberger was still upset, but eventually he accepted that packing books is an act of sharing—with the added benefit of diminishing the ego. And what good preparation this would be for the many years when he and I were the only two people doing this work! Those years in the early 70s, were some of the best times in our life together. We were the first volunteers of the Research Centre of Kabbalah. We were enveloped by Light as we boxed up and shipped copies of Rav Ashlag's books.

The important lesson to derive from this is that a kabbalist doesn't just practice by praying and studying, but also in everything he does. Rav Brandwein was the first person to help my husband understand that the Light is not only revealed when you steep yourself in wisdom. It also enters when you're teaching, and when you're performing acts of kindness and generosity for the benefit of others. Philip Gruberger was smart and capable, and he thought he could absorb more than most, yet this was an opportunity for him to see that there was Light to reveal in the ordinary world of everyday activity.

He did learn quickly, although some insights took longer to acquire. When he came to Israel, the Rav felt an unquenchable thirst to be with the source of his transformation—Rav Brandwein. Unfortunately, the Rav was oblivious to the fact that this evoked a lot of jealousy from Rav Brandwein's family, which he later regretted. At the time, all he wanted was to connect to the Light through his soul mate, and being a businessman he assumed that any obstacles he met could be resolved through negotiation.

Along came this American with a lot of money who said, "Go out and buy yourself whatever you want. Just leave me alone with my teacher." Rav Brandwein's family accepted the gifts because in those days in Israel no one had much in the way of material prosperity, but eventually this caused so much animosity that during Erev Rosh Hashanah, Rav Brandwein would not allow my husband to pray with him. "I have to spend the holiday with my family," Rav Brandwein explained. My husband went back to his apartment depressed and miserable. Later he would say this Rosh Hashanah was the worst of his life, which prompted me to ask him, "Because you didn't spend the holiday with Rav Brandwein or because you didn't get your way?"

The truth is, probably both. He had been acting out of arrogance and pride. Up to this time, he had always found a way to get whatever he wanted. He felt so wounded by Rav Brandwein's denial that he was ready to return to New

York. This is when he learned a foundational principle of Kabbalah. We are Vessels whose very essence is this Desire to Receive. If we take energy by receiving Light directly for ourselves alone without considering others through bribery in this particular case we feel pain and shame. It's the spiritual work required to transform our Desire to Receive for Ourselves Alone into a Desire to Receive for the Purpose of Sharing that allows us to receive the fulfillment of the Light. This is the way we become similar in form to the Light of the Creator. But this is not an easy lesson to learn, especially for a successful businessman, and it took a while for my husband to absorb it.

The Endless Story

Before the beginning, there was a dimension of existence that Kabbalah calls the Endless World, made up of two aspects of energy. The first was the Light—an infinite and constant desire to share. This was the source of goodness, a divine, life-giving force beyond our comprehension. Kabbalists say we cannot understand the infinite nature of the Creator with our finite mind but we can begin to understand the qualities of the Creator, which include all manner of fulfillment.

Since the Light wanted to impart its boundless fulfillment, a receiver of that Light and abundance—a Vessel—was created. The Vessel—the second aspect of energy—was a form of infinite receiving. This flow of energy from the

Light to the Vessel took place in a realm of existence that lay beyond the confines of time and space. The Endless World, was a state of complete harmony. Until something happened.

Although the Vessel was created to receive, once it was imbued with the outpouring of the Creator's essence, the Vessel began to desire to be like the Creator, to be a source of giving. In the Endless World, the original Vessel no longer found it fulfilling to be the effect; it wanted to share and thereby to become the cause. This new energy that the Vessel was experiencing is called Bread of Shame—the result of receiving something when there is no active desire for it or effort expended to earn it. Bread of Shame created a challenge in paradise.

So what did the Vessel do? It pushed back and resisted the Light. Since the Creator's only intention was to fulfill the Vessel, the Creator then withdrew the Light, which constricted into a single, infinitely small point. The utter darkness that followed was unbearable for the Vessel, so the Light rushed back in at full force. But the Vessel wasn't ready. It shattered, exploding into an illimitable number of fragments, thus creating all the souls of mankind as well as time, space, motion, and the physical universe as we know it today. Science calls this moment the Big Bang.

Bread of Shame was the reason for the creation of our world. The Creator initiated this process to fulfill the Vessel's desire to share, to create, to be the cause. Our purpose in this world is to learn to be more like that Creator, and by so doing draw the Creator's essence more fully into our lives without resulting in Bread of Shame.

This is a good opportunity to talk about ego. Many years later, the Rav would call the sanctuary at the Kabbalah Centre the "War Room." Why? Because for a kabbalist the only real enemy is the force of ego, and the greatest battles against it are fought and won inside of us. "Our prayers," he would say, "are the means by which we fortify the Light of our soul so that we have the strength to battle our own egos and the internal demons," he called Satan's armada. Prayer is the way of connecting to the Light that can help us defeat the ego so we can expand and elevate our consciousness.

What is ego? It's the reactive, self-centered, small-minded voice that shouts over the quiet voice of our souls. Why does it exist? So we can use our free will to choose the voice of our soul over the louder clamor of the Desire to Receive for the Self Alone. This choice removes Bread of Shame from the source of our fulfillment. The Light of the Creator sends us trials because we need them. In those trials we always have a choice of who we'll become, depending on which inner voice we listen to.

The challenge we face from the ego helps us focus on the transformation of our desire, the evolution of our consciousness. The war within helps us change, grow, and expand our awareness. For kabbalists, the Armageddon before the coming of the Messianic age is a war of thoughts. In this struggle a single act of kindness performed in resistance to an evil inclination reveals more Light than we can imagine.

Kabbalah teaches that the problems we encounter in our lives are specifically designed for our benefit by the most profound algorithm, the Lightforce of God. We may rage in self-pity against our troubles or in anger at people we perceive as having wounded us but without adversity we could not rise up to receive the blessings of the Creator. So, as my husband wrestled with his ego that Rosh Hashanah eve, he came to realize that Rav Brandwein's denial of him was not the issue. No, it was his own desire to receive for himself alone that was causing him pain.

By thwarting Philip Gruberger, his teacher was showing him what it meant to humble his ego and silence its voice. It's one thing to read about this principle in books and another entirely to act on it. Reading, studying, and learning for its own sake doesn't necessarily translate into a spiritual life. That night my husband discovered the true meaning of humility. And he changed.

* * *

Only a few years after meeting Rav Brandwein, my husband dedicated himself completely to the wisdom of Kabbalah. Later, when he and I met again, we made it our purpose to teach it to everyone we used to call it *lehafitz Kabbalah* (to spread Kabbalah). He adored Rav Brandwein.

Rav Brandwein was a humble man. In his own mind his greatest accomplishment was that he was a servant to Rav Ashlag and a disseminator of his teachings. Despite his humility, however, he was an amazing scholar who translated sections of the Zohar and commentary that Rav Ashlag had not completed before he left this world. Rav Brandwein was clearly a spiritual giant, yet his view of himself and the way he interacted with others was that of a simple, caring being.

Rav Brandwein could trace his bloodline back to King David. In addition, he was a descendant of the esteemed Rav Dov Ber of Mezeritch (also known as the Maggid of Mezeritch), a great spiritual leader in Russia during the late 18th century who took on the mantle of the Baal Shem Tov. Yet Rav Brandwein was also the embodiment of *ahavat chinam*—unconditional and selfless love—a trait that my husband would come to embrace. This love was an important part of Rav Brandwein's teachings.

Early in their relationship, he showed Philip Gruberger an introduction he had written to an 18-volume compilation of the Ari's writings. In this essay Rav Brandwein used the term *lezulat*. This word has many meanings, and usually it's translated as "outside" or "other than," but in a kabbalistic context it means reaching a level of love that takes a person outside of himself—to love for no reason.

Rav Brandwein believed that spreading the word of the Creator did not require correcting the flaws of others. One simply needed to find the deepest place within themselves and from this place share love; spirituality would follow naturally. This is the kind of love that my husband felt for his teacher—the spark he received *from* his teacher, which he later gave to all of his students. They, in turn, became teachers themselves to share it with the world.

Rav Brandwein possessed a remarkable gift for reclaiming the souls of those who had become disaffected. He imparted spirituality to all who met him by embodying the truths of the Creator. My husband believed Rav Brandwein was able to do this because he saw the Light in each person. Their exterior—how a man or woman appeared or acted—was irrelevant to him.

"Do not look at the container but search for what is inside," Rav Brandwein instructed during their evenings together. "Everyone is worth our time and love. Give people breathing space. Listen to them and honor what they have to say. Respect everyone without focusing on or being influenced by their outer appearance. Above all, make enough room in your heart to love each and every person without thinking about what you will get in return." *Lezulat*.

Many years later, the Rav's extraordinary capacity to love helped to heal Eitan Yardeni, one of our teachers who had become depressed because he was struggling with a great deal of physical pain. Only in his twenties, he was ready to give up. But one Friday night after prayers, the Rav turned toward Eitan, concerned about how he was feeling. "In his eyes, in his face," Eitan explained, "I felt that the Rav was absorbing the pain. He cared about me more than I cared about myself, and that was a turning point for me. His love awakened me to the desire to be better and to heal."

* * *

Because of his open and accepting heart, Rav Brandwein felt comfortable approaching almost anyone. Consequently, many people from all walks of life loved him, including the people of the Histadrut, the Israeli Labor Union made up of truckers, dockworkers, machinists, and bus drivers who believed in the state of Israel but had no interest in religion. Even Levi Eshkol, the Israeli Prime Minister at that time, frequently sought Rav Brandwein's counsel.

"So many people in the world today have lost their faith," Rav Brandwein explained to my husband as he described his goals. "The people of the world cannot carry on without spirituality. I do not understand why in all this time someone has not brought forth the great and obvious remedy to this problem, Kabbalah, and the great book of Kabbalah, the Holy Zohar. Instead, the very scholars who have access to this healing medicine either withhold it or write inaccuracies about it, which make it impossible for the average person to return to spirituality."

My husband watched his teacher bring people to spirituality without the slightest hint of superiority or the least bit of pressure. Rav Brandwein had learned this approach from Rav Ashlag, who had taught him, "There is no coercion in spirituality." Rav Brandwein believed that if the Creator of all things, who wants only good for us, holds back Light and fulfillment to allow us the free will to choose Him, who are we to push someone toward spirituality? If people are not ready to recognize the deeper workings of the universe, forcing them to do so might even be harmful.

Because their souls were so aligned, Rav Brandwein and Philip Gruberger spent many hours together during the day in addition to their nighttime studies. They went on long drives across Israel. This allowed my husband to observe his teacher in action, and to see the many ways in which Rav Brandwein served as a living embodiment of Kabbalah.

The two men were among the first to regularly visit the gravesites of the *tzadikim*, the spiritual masters. They paid many visits to Meron to pray at the grave of Rav Shimon Bar Yochai, especially on the holiday of Lag B'Omer, which celebrates the day he left this physical plane as well as the revelation of the Zohar.

Each kabbalist's grave represented a different aspect of spiritual energy. Some inspired a longing for enlightenment, others prompted solutions for problems, while still others advanced the merit we need to find our soul mate. Teacher and student would also travel to the Idra Rabba, the site on the way to Meron, where Rav Shimon and his followers revealed the Zohar. Many years later it became a tradition at the Kabbalah Centre for students to make pilgrimages to these gravesites as well.

The two men also traveled while Rav Brandwein fulfilled his role as Chief Rabbi of the Histadrut. The organization, which included all of Israel's trade unions, was more than a million members strong. Interestingly, this association pointedly ignored Judaism, and some of its members opposed religion of any kind. The Histadrut's annual dinner dance, for example, was scheduled on the holiest of Holy Days, Yom Kippur, a day set aside by observant Jews for repentance and contemplation. Rav Brandwein's position in the organization was seen as a provocation and created a hullabaloo among Orthodox, Conservative, and Reform Jews. His involvement was interpreted as his condoning atheism and even heresy. Rav Brandwein's wife feared their children would never marry because the family's reputation was so tainted by his involvement.

Established in 1920, during the British Mandate for Palestine, the Histadrut was one of Israel's most powerful institutions from the 1950s to the 1970s, when socialism was prevalent in Israeli society. David Ben-Gurion, who would become the first Prime Minister of Israel, was elected the organization's first secretary in 1921. For a time, the Histadrut was Israel's largest employer, but as Israeli society began to move away from socialism, the group went into decline. Still, in 1983, it had 1,600,000 members, more than a third of Israel's total population at that time. In addition to secretly teaching Kabbalah at night, Rav Brandwein was playing a highly visible role in the wellbeing of his country as the Histadrut's Chief Rabbi.

The Rav's master was also laying the groundwork for what would later become a complete break with the Orthodox view of Kabbalah. His teacher, Rav Ashlag, had sought to make the wisdom more accessible. Rav Brandwein was the first kabbalist to engage with everyday people, not just fellow rabbis. At functions and conferences he shared basic principles of Kabbalah without identifying them as such. He came in through the back door.

The Rav liked to tell the story of a visit the two men paid to a munitions factory in the town of Yokne'am that employed about 21,000 workers. As they walked through the door, the factory manager came running over to Rav Brandwein. My husband could see from his clothes that this man was not Orthodox, and that this was a secular facility. Rav Brandwein, on the other hand, was dressed as always, as a *chusid*—an Orthodox man in a black coat and hat with a beard and *peyois* (side locks). But despite their outward differences, the manager greeted Rav Brandwein with a hearty embrace.

Philip Gruberger was curious about this interaction, so later he asked the manager, "Tell me, how is it that you feel such a connection to him?"

The manager replied, "He is not just a rabbi; he is a *Mekubal*." This Hebrew word is used with reverence to describe a holy person, a sage. My husband was floored that this clearly secular person would hold his teacher in such high regard.

During this visit, Rav Brandwein told my husband a story about the first time he walked into this plant. When he visited the dining hall, he saw most of the workers eating together but off to one side, a small group was having lunch, segregated from the rest. So he asked the manager, "Why aren't all the workers eating together?"

The manager replied, "Well, the people in the corner are religious; they only eat kosher food. Our kitchen isn't kosher, so out of respect to them and to prevent their food from being contaminated, I made a special place for them."

Rav Brandwein understood this logic, and he could have simply accepted the situation. But he was astute enough to recognize that this kind of separation might, in the long run, perpetuate more harm than good.

"It is obvious that you care deeply for your workers and have great respect for them," he said to the manager kindly. "But unfortunately the solution is creating an even greater problem. Although your workers who observe *kashrut*, the Jewish laws that govern kosher foods, can now safely eat their own food, they are effectively isolated from everyone else in the factory. The religious and non-religious do not mix and because of this they are unlikely to form friendships. In trying to solve the *kashrut* issue, you may have driven people apart, and this can only be bad for worker morale in the whole factory."

The manager quickly grasped the point and asked Rav Brandwein to propose a better solution. Rav Brandwein replied, "Listen, if non-religious people eat kosher food, it's not a big problem for them—people who eat non-kosher can eat kosher too. But you know, the reverse is not true. People who observe kosher laws are forbidden from eating non-kosher food. I think the solution is for the Histadrut to build a kosher kitchen here—I am happy to donate some of my own money for this—and then everyone will be able to eat together. We speak about unity in our country, and this would help us be unified." Rav Brandwein did not have much money, so the manager understood the significance of his offer.

Sure enough, the entire munitions factory became a kosher facility, and everyone was able to sit and eat together in peace and harmony. This story contained an important lesson: compromise is not always the best solution because each party loses a little. The Rav learned from his teacher to always seek a third option—one that reveals the Light and allows everyone to keep their views intact. When the Rav included this story in his book, Education of a Kabbalist, he said, "What I saw with my teacher and the people of the Labor Union was love that transcended self-interest and personal need; a love that had no agenda, no self-consideration. This was just pure goodness flowing unconditionally." *Lezulat*.

Eventually, every factory in Israel associated with the Histadrut had a kosher kitchen thanks to Rav Brandwein's vision of unity and love. In gratitude for his efforts on behalf of their workers, the Histadrut provided Rav Brandwein with funds to allocate to people in need. One day, my husband was waiting in an anteroom outside Rav Brandwein's office when a disgruntled man stormed out, ranting about what a horrible person Rav Brandwein was. When the tirade ended and the man left, Philip Gruberger went in to see his teacher.

"It boggles my mind," my husband said. "Here you are giving money to this needy man so he can finish his project, yet he can't wait to tell a total stranger all kinds of nasty things about you. What's going on?"

Rav Brandwein simply replied, "I must not have done him enough good yet."

This teaching really sank in, and much later in the Rav's life I could see it come to fruition. When non-Jewish students began studying at the Centre, rabbis in the greater Jewish community wrote scurrilous articles about the Rav in the local newspaper, hoping to drive away our Jewish students. Our teachers wanted to publish a strong response. They drafted an article and gave it to the Rav for his blessing, but after having read it, he became quiet. Then he said, "We are not going to do anything. I'm sorry that you wasted your time on this instead of revealing Light by studying or helping people. You have been busy with the work of Satan. With the darkness."

The teachers asked, "Why, Rav? What did we do?"

"Don't you see that this is what the opponent wants from us? To be busy with negative things. Please focus your energies on bringing Light to the world."

"So what are we going to say to these rabbis?" they wanted to know.

"Nothing," replied the Rav. "Just be busy with peace."

The Rav had little tolerance for wasting time. He wanted to focus on the things that mattered, and getting caught up in a public spat was not one of them.

The Rav told me many other stories about his teacher, each of which contributed in some way to his own evolution from Philip Gruberger to Rav Berg. One important incident occurred in 1967, shortly before the Six Day War between Israel and its neighbors Egypt, Syria, and Jordan. On that day, my husband accompanied Rav Brandwein to the town of Tiberius on the shores of Lake Kinneret, in the north of Israel, near the Golan Heights. There they prayed together.

On the way home, Rav Brandwein said, "You have no idea what we've done for the people of Tiberius today." My husband was mystified by this statement but not long afterwards, Syria fired a number of missiles at Tiberius. Only one struck the town—and that one landed in the cemetery. No one was injured. Philip Gruberger was certain that Tiberius had been spared because Rav Brandwein had protected it with his prayers. In this way my husband learned about the importance of prayer and *kavanah* (intention).

Rav Brandwein brought Light to the darkness around Tiberius and the town was shielded from harm. This moment became the basis of the Rav's certainty that if human beings apply their consciousness to a specific end, aided by the tools of Kabbalah, they can reshape destiny. It was a seminal moment in the Rav's practical education.

I could see this certainty at work after September 11, 2001. The Rav felt tremendous pain over this terrible tragedy. He believed that if more Light had been revealed in the world then 9/11 could have been prevented. This strengthened his resolve to do more. Shortly thereafter, Kabbalah Centre volunteers began handing out free single volume mini-Zohars to everyone at the Marriott Marquis, the hotel that served as a temporary home for firefighters and other emergency workers at Ground Zero. We posted a toll-free number for people who desired the protection of the Zohar, and once planes were flying again we went to

New York airports to distribute Zohars to flight attendants and others. Whatever the Rav could do to reveal the Light, he would do.

Although the Rav's master dressed in the same religious attire that might have been worn a thousand years earlier, Rav Brandwein was remarkably modern and open, and put human dignity first in every situation. He couldn't have worked for the Histadrut if he hadn't been tolerant. He had a spirit that understood and respected other people even though his particular preference was to live the way he did. This openness caused Rav Brandwein problems within his family. His son-in-law would bring his own food to eat at Rav Brandwein's house because he feared that some of the Histadrut's anti-religious sentiment might be rubbing off on Rav Brandwein. He might not be kosher enough!

The more time Rabbi Gruberger spent with Rav Brandwein the less attention he paid to his businesses. Not surprisingly, they were suffering. Once he wrote his teacher a letter from New York in which he shared, "You know, I have a lot of serious business problems happening at this moment."

But Rav Brandwein replied in essence, "Everybody has issues on their own spiritual playing field." And the closer Philip Gruberger became to his teacher and the study of Kabbalah, the further away he moved from his family and community in New York. Rav Brandwein could have said, "Listen. Go home and stay with your wife and children. We'll correspond through the mail," but he didn't. He realized the deep importance of their connection, and he wanted Philip Gruberger to be with him. Early on in their relationship Rav Brandwein said to my husband, "You will be the one to follow me." As great kabbalists do, he had a gift for looking into the future.

In 1968, Rivka and the Gruberger children moved from New York to Israel to be closer to their husband and father, and to Rivka's extended family. They lived in an apartment near the ultra-Orthodox Mea She'arim neighborhood in Jerusalem on Rahov Nevi'im—the "Street of the Prophets." This long road runs through modern Jerusalem toward the Old City. Many people walk from this area to the Wailing or Western Wall (the Kotel) to pray on Shabbat. But even though they were now all living in the same city, Philip Gruberger and his family were rarely together.

By this time, Rav Brandwein had left Tel Aviv and moved to the Old City of Jerusalem into a house provided by the Histadrut in gratitude for his years of service. In fact, after the Six-Day War, Rav Brandwein had the honor of being the first Israeli citizen permitted to live in this very special area of Jerusalem. My husband spent most of his time with his teacher in this place of study. On several occasions he brought his younger sons to visit. Naftali, my husband's youngest son from his marriage to Rivka, still remembers being blessed by Rav Brandwein. He and his brother used to walk to their great uncle's house in the Old City every Shabbat.

Once Rav Brandwein connected with my husband, he realized that this connection between himself and Philip Gruberger was the reason for everything else that had gone before. This man had married his niece so student and master could meet and study together. Indeed, several weeks before his death, Rav Brandwein told my husband that his gift to the world would be explaining Kabbalah in such a way that all people would understand it. He also warned his student that he would encounter a great deal of adversity and opposition.

Rav Brandwein was right on all counts.

* * *

During the seven years he studied with Rav Brandwein, the Rav became increasingly absorbed in learning and disseminating Kabbalah. Since it was not openly studied at the time in the United States, my husband distributed the books Rav Brandwein had published to influential Orthodox rabbis. The Rav believed that if he could interest the leaders of the Orthodox and ultra-Orthodox communities in New York in the works of his teachers, perhaps their devotees would become followers of Rav Ashlag and Rav Brandwein as well.

During one of Philip Gruberger infrequent trips to New York to tend to his businesses, he decided to devote a small space in his insurance office on Remsen Street in Brooklyn to disseminating kabbalistic texts and to fundraising for Rav Brandwein's school and its publishing activities. This office became the National Institute for Research in Kabbalah. The Rav became so committed to this effort that between 1965 and 1969 he lived half the time in Israel and half the time in the United States—even after his family had relocated to Jerusalem to be there with him. During this period, he visited every single influential rabbi in New York.

Meanwhile, Rav Brandwein completed his translation of the *Hashmatot HaZohar* ("Addendum of the Zohar") and although the Histadrut had funded the printing, Rav Brandwein now needed to sell it. Unfortunately, few people in Israel were interested in buying his books, so the Rav took a thousand volumes to New York to sell. Although hardly anyone who bought them could even read the Zohar, this was an important first step. Even the Rav could not have imagined what it would lead to in the future. Twenty years after my husband and Rav Brandwein struggled to sell the *Hashmatot HaZohar*, the Kabbalah Centre published a magnificent edition of the Zohar together with *The Sulam*. Our first printing was 25,000 copies.

* * *

It's a simple fact that kabbalists have always been short of money. Rav Shmuel Vital, whose father studied with the great Rav Isaac Luria, wrote about this problem, as did many others after him. Rav Brandwein's own teacher, Rav Ashlag, once wanted to publish an encyclopedia of all the concepts and terminologies of Kabbalah but this ambitious idea languished for lack of funds. Fundraising was a constant theme in the lives of Rav Brandwein and my husband. Numerous letters between them while he was in

New York spoke to Philip Gruberger's efforts to solve this pressing problem.

Financial difficulties had arisen decades earlier, when Rav Ashlag founded his Yeshiva. Times were hard, and Rav Ashlag himself was impoverished. The Great Depression had been followed by constant wars in Israel that undermined any real hope of prosperity in the country. It's not surprising then, that during their first encounter and without even knowing him, Rav Brandwein asked Philip Gruberger, "Can you support my yeshiva?" The need was great.

There were taxes to pay, as well as various fees, and wages for the Yeshiva students who collected a small salary that allowed them to study fulltime. People participating in the daily *minyan*—the quorum of ten men over the age of thirteen required for traditional Jewish public worship—also expected payment. It was common practice in Orthodox circles that scholars would be paid to study Torah.

I have always been fascinated by the ways that money and spirituality are tied together. Today, the Kabbalah Centre continues to be unbashful about the need to raise funds for the work we do. At that time, however, the Rav took it upon himself to fund the printing and distribution of books. He also hired translators and editors to create a Modern Hebrew version of Volume 1 of the *Talmud Eser Sefirot* ("Study of the Ten Luminous Emanations," TLE), one of Rav Ashlag's two great kabbalistic works. Rav Ashlag's relatives sued Rav Brandwein to stop the project but eventually they came to a mutually acceptable agreement and TLE was published in Modern Hebrew. We can only thank the Creator that it did not share the fate of Rav Ashlag's numerous other manuscripts, which to this day remain in storage, many greatly damaged.

The grand-sounding National Institute for Research in Kabbalah became the seat of the Rav's fundraising efforts. He leveraged everything he could—his personal, political, and business relationships as well as connections with others whom he had met along the way—to help Rav Brandwein realize his vision. He still had ties to various great rabbis in New York whom he had supported before 1962, so he asked them about donating money so that Yeshivat Kol Yehuda could print more books. He was even successful in interesting influential individuals outside the Jewish faith. Cardinal Spellman of the Archdiocese of New York agreed to raise funds for the Yeshiva.

Aside from appealing directly to potential donors, my husband and Rav Brandwein sought other ways to collect donations. In 1968, as Rav Brandwein was readying himself to print the second part of *Tikkunei Zohar*, he suggested to Philip Gruberger that he offer to print dedication pages at the front of the books in memory of parents and other relatives. "This is what we used to do with the Zohar of our master, the Baal HaSulam (the author of the Sulam commentary), may his merit protect us," Rav Brandwein wrote, referring to Rav Ashlag and his work.

The Rav approached these challenges with an unwavering sense of commitment. "As long as God gives me strength," he wrote to his teacher, "I will work with all of that strength, giving over completely my soul to do this work." No longer the business tycoon and political force he once was, now all he cared about was making enough money so that he could support his family and spread the wisdom of Kabbalah.

One of the Rav's few unpublished letters to his teacher that I possess gives us a taste of their struggle, the financial difficulties they encountered, and the Rav's complete devotion to his teacher and their work.

> *July 24th, 1968*
>
> *To the honor of my teacher, my rabbi, a man of many actions, the love of my soul, a person from whom I can never separate myself, my beloved, my teacher, Rabbi Yehuda Tzvi Brandwein, and regards to his wife, Leah.*
>
> *I'm sending a check for $500, and I trust that the Creator will send me the money, because right now I don't have it. I have debts, and I hope that we will be successful in what we do. I know that you don't understand why I don't have money, but the reality is my money is invested either in lots or in hotels, and right now I don't have income, even for my family. But I trust that the assistance from the Creator will come in an instant, from a place we don't even expect.*
>
> *If you want to know why some of the things we've done together didn't succeed, I think I know.*

It's because of my spiritual shortcomings and negative things that I've done. And therefore, the most important thing is for me to purify my soul. With the help of the Creator.

I can never separate from you. And I look forward to the secrets that I will continue learning from you. But we are dealing with deep and pure things, and of course there will be many obstacles in the way. To do it in a small way is not enough. I think the Creator wants us to do great things because this is great work.

In that same letter, my husband described a business venture that eventually soured. Rav Brandwein's grandson had contracted polio. My husband did whatever he could and searched everywhere to find a cure or at the very least to relieve the child's suffering. In this instance, he found a doctor who had invented some kind of equipment that might be helpful. My husband invested in it but the project ended in failure and created tension between Philip Gruberger and his teacher.

In another unpublished letter sent nearly a month later, on the 27th of Av, 1968 (August 21, 1968), my husband shares his deep commitment:

To the beloved of my soul, my teacher, Yehuda Tzvi Brandwein. I was very happy to speak to you on the phone. There's nothing else to update. I ask that you write me a letter every week because your teachings are what give me life. Every day, I study at least three hours, and everywhere I go, I take the book Ten Luminous Emanations, not to waste any time. I hope that the fundraising letter will help and we will be able to raise some money. I am working with all of my strength. This is all I really want to deal with as long as I am able.

I know that the Creator, with your blessing, will bring success, because we know the Creator listens even to the poor, and to the righteous, and pious person of course. The Creator will hear your prayer.

Shabbat Shalom.

Desiring to see you soon, to hear your teachings face-to-face.

* * *

After several years of his devoting himself to Rav Brandwein, Yeshivat Kol Yehuda, the publications, and the Kabbalistic teachings, my husband's financial empire collapsed. Its slow unraveling accelerated in 1965 when the Rav went all in with money and political support for Paul Screvane's bid to become mayor of New York. Abe Beame defeated Screvane in the Democratic primary but then lost to the Republican, John Lindsay. Not only did Philip Gruberger lose the funds he had contributed to the campaign, but in the absence of a Democratic administration, my husband suddenly lost much of his clout.

If his candidate had won, he would have been likely to get more insurance contracts from the city but that hope was gone. With the Rav's focus and vast energy trained elsewhere, the situation only worsened from there. By late 1968, a few months before Rav Brandwein's death, it was clear that the businesses were no longer sustainable. My husband often told a prophetic story about their final demise.

He and Rav Brandwein were walking along the narrow, winding paths of the Old Jewish Cemetery that spreads out below the city of Safed. They went there once or twice a month, if possible, to visit the graves of the righteous. On that particular day, they were hiking down the mountain from the Ari's deep turquoise tomb to another grave at the base of the mountain, that of Rav Shimon Bar Yochai's father-in-law, Rav Pinchas ben Yair. Along the way they stopped at the spot where Rav Brandwein's great-grandparents had been buried. As Philip Gruberger and his teacher approached it, they noticed a black scorpion crawling on the grave.

Rav Brandwein gave his cane to my husband and said, "If you kill the scorpion, all of your financial problems will go away." My husband crushed the poisonous insect. And in the ensuing days his remaining business enterprises completely collapsed. When the Rav told this story he said, "I didn't know then what Rav Brandwein meant when he said my problems would go away." Then he laughed. "Now I see that when I killed the scorpion, the business was completely finished. I suppose I had to lose my money so as not to be distracted by business concerns, and thus be able to devote myself wholly to spreading Kabbalah's great truths."

* * *

In the early spring of 1969, Philip Gruberger was several months shy of his forty-second birthday. He had been studying with his master for seven years. In March of that year, my husband entered his teacher's study late one night and saw that his face was shining, as he described it, "with the splendor of the Firmament." Rav Brandwein had just finished the Hebrew translation of the last volume of *Talmud Eser Sefirot* ("Study of the Ten Luminous Emanations").

A few short weeks later, on April 2, the first night of Passover, Philip Gruberger arrived at Rav Brandwein's house for the Seder. For the second time in their seven-year relationship, Rav Brandwein met him at the door and said, "It would be best if we were not together tonight. My family has had a big argument about it." With tears in his eyes, Rav Brandwein said, "Go home." Pesach had been a joyous holiday for Philip Gruberger and Rav Brandwein—I have photos showing the two of them baking matzos together in previous years—but not this year.

Three evenings later, my husband visited the Brandwein home again. This time he found his teacher weak and in bed, but again absolutely radiant. Philip Gruberger could feel that Rav Brandwein's work in this world was coming to an end. Apparently, he'd had a heart attack, perhaps brought on by his refusal to take his blood thinners because they were *chametz* (not Kosher for Passover). Whatever the reason, it was clear that Rav Brandwein was leaving this Earthly plane.

Philip Gruberger wanted desperately to be with his teacher then but the family objected and turned him away. I can understand this. My husband felt that he was Rav Brandwein's son; he thought he belonged at his side, yet this was not the time to argue. Acceding to the family's wishes, he left. In fact, he ran into traffic, looking frantically for an ambulance to direct to the house. He was still out on the street when his teacher left the world.

My husband was distraught. The fact that Rav Brandwein—the soul mate from whom he had wished never to be parted—had just died, was more than he could bear. But being denied access to him during those final moments was shattering—so much so that he was never able to really talk about it. I know that when people are traumatized, the language part of the brain shuts down, and they actually have no words to describe their ordeal. This is what happened to my husband on that difficult night. Whenever he broached the subject in the years that followed, he would just stop at this point as tears welled up. It did give him solace, however, to remember that when the Ari died, his chosen student, Chaim Vital, also arrived minutes after the passing and did not witness his teacher's death.

Still, at the time of Rav Brandwein's transition my husband was devastated.

By Jewish tradition, there is little time to bury someone once they pass. The family had to quickly choose a plot from among three options: In the city of Safed, near the resting place of the Ari at the Old Jewish Cemetery (where they had killed the scorpion), where other members of the Brandwein family were also interred; a plot at the cemetery on the Mount of Olives that had been off limits to Jews until the Six Day War in 1967; or a space next to Rav Ashlag's tomb at the largest cemetery in Jerusalem called Har HaMenuchot, which translates to "Mount of Those Who Are Resting." This cemetery is situated on a hilltop at the western edge of the city adjacent to Giv'at Shaul, overlooking the neighborhood where Rav Ashlag had taught Rav Brandwein so many years earlier.

Rav Brandwein's family was leaning toward the Mount of Olives, but here Philip Gruberger was able to influence their decision. He said, "You know, I really think he would like to be with his teacher." This was one of the few pieces of advice they accepted from him. Rav Brandwein's body was laid to rest beside Rav Ashlag's on Har HaMenuchot, on the outskirts of Jerusalem.

My husband stayed for *shloshim*, the 30-day period of mourning following burial. There was no shiva, the seven days of mourning, because Rav Brandwein died during Passover. Distant from his own family and bereft of his beloved teacher and soul mate, the Rav felt there was nothing more for him in Israel. So in early May, 1969, about a month after Rav Brandwein's death, Philip Gruberger left Jerusalem and made his way back to New York alone, a lost and broken man.

CHAPTER 4:

TWO WORLDS COLLIDE: I ENTER THE PICTURE

Who would have believed that not three weeks later, my former boss would be engaged in an intense conversation with me over bagels, lox, and scrambled eggs at Ratner's, the famous kosher deli on the lower Eastside of Manhattan? We were approaching the summer of 1969. A series of snapshots of that time in America would show continuous protests against the war in Vietnam; free love, wild music, and plentiful drugs at a farm in Woodstock, in upstate New York; Neil Armstrong's first footsteps on the moon; the horrific Manson murders in Los Angeles; Ted Kennedy's unraveling at Chappaquiddick. The year before this, the Beatles had released *The White Album*, the Stones urged us to show "Sympathy for the Devil," and the Doors pushed us to "Break on Through" as the sexual revolution, spawned by the advent of birth control pills, turned the notion of morality on its head.

Baby Boomers, now in their late teens and early twenties, were questioning authority as never before in history. No longer was it acceptable to follow the rules just because things had always been done a certain way—tradition had lost its hold. This generation wanted to know the "Why?" not just the "How?" or the "What?" They thought freely and loved freely; they experimented with hallucinogens and new forms of religious observance. Indeed, they spurned rote observance of established Judeo-Christian religious rituals as meaningless, and interest in what soon became New Age spirituality began accelerating.

Suddenly, people were talking about reincarnation, karma, Heaven, astrology, out-of-body experiences, isolation tanks, psychics, psychedelics, Zen Buddhism, astral projection, and near-death visions of Light. Countless spiritual seekers embarked on a quest for meaning and enlightenment. All kinds of prayer, meditation, and consciousness raising techniques became common in the business world, at universities, and in rural communes where hippies had gathered to live and love.

The Rav, insulated by his observant religious community, was hardly touched by the societal upheaval of 1969. But I had been a seeker for some time. I watched as society started reshaping itself all around me, as young people challenged every boundary. Indeed, thanks to the musical *Hair*, people were singing about the dawning of the Age of Aquarius—the full flowering of the counterculture was going mainstream.

In retrospect, it seems as if the universe was providing fertile soil for the seed of the Kabbalah Centre, though it would take years for it to bear fruit. The Rav was too respectful of the tradition he'd been given to teach, and I was too young for us to suddenly become a "pair of great marketers taking advantage of the times," as we've sometimes been portrayed. Instead, I believe the collision of our worlds was preordained to coincide with this historic moment of disruption and transformation.

Let me explain. The Rav would say, "People think Jerusalem is holy because the Temple is there but spiritually we understand that the reverse is true. The Temple is in Jerusalem because that holy ground is a portal for spiritual energy." The Temple was built as an instrument to manifest, radiate, and share that energy with the rest of the world.

So it was with our connection. A great spiritual ferment in the universe brought us together to create the modern Kabbalah movement. When you look at our lives—the Rav with his hidebound history and me with my chaotic childhood—it was highly unlikely that we would have ever met or connected on a soul level had it not been predestined. There was something Godly about our union. The universe brought us together. The universe made this happen. The universe was ready to manifest the Kabbalah Centre.

So there we were at Ratner's, an Orthodox rabbi in his early 40s dressed in a long black frock coat, black hat, and beard—and no, he wasn't in anyway being ironic—and a young mother of two little girls in her late 20s wearing a miniskirt and boots. We were completely absorbed in our life-altering conversation and oblivious to our reflections in the wall-to-wall mirrors surrounding us or the curious glances of the other patrons in the restaurant.

Nine years had passed since my first encounter with Rabbi Philip Gruberger, and he seemed an entirely different person. I'd never been crazy about the guy who was my boss at the insurance company. Yes, he had done a lot of good things in business and for his community but in my opinion, he was also somewhat arrogant and authoritarian. Religious, yes, but not spiritual, and I had been put off by that. Now, although he was still strictly observant, he seemed to have softened. His heart was open, and he was humbler and more willing to listen. He was sensitive and in tune. And he was much, much more spiritual.

All in all, it was a remarkable metamorphosis.

This time it was clear that we had made a soul mate connection, although by all outward appearances we were the unlikeliest pair. I did not know it at the time, but Rav Isaac Luria (the Ari), had written that a soul mate marriage can be identified as two people who join from "across the sea." This means its partners come together from different cultures, not from a shared community; the connection is soul-based. This was certainly true in our relationship. In contrast to the Rav, who had had a stable home and a secure childhood, my early life was chaotic, unpredictable, and utterly lacking in structure or religious education.

I grew up without a father; he died before I was a year old. My young mother, Beatrice, wanted a life for herself, so she was rarely home. I lived with my grandmother Rose. We were very close, and with her help, I raised myself. And no, there were no pieces of chocolate or glasses of milk waiting for me when I got home from school in the afternoon. Eventually, my mother married my stepdad, and I moved in with them. They had a daughter together who was twelve years younger than me.

My life should have settled down with this marriage but it didn't. My stepdad worked seasonally as a hotel manager in Miami Beach, Florida. Every September, I would start school in New York but by November we would move to Miami. Then, back to New York in the spring as the weather warmed up, the hotels shut down, and snowbirds fled the heat by heading north. Each time we moved I was placed in a new school; I attended thirteen different schools by eighth grade.

It was an itinerant, confusing existence for a child. I never experienced the stability of what I imagined to be a normal home. Due to lack of continuity and parental oversight, I was five years behind in reading, which meant I was always in deep trouble at school. My classmates teased me, calling me retarded.

One night when I was only ten, some neighborhood bullies threw me into a pit in a construction site. I couldn't climb out. Trapped in the dark and cold, afraid that I would die, I started crying. As horrible as it was, that incident became a positive turning point in my life. At one point that night I distinctly heard a voice. We all hear voices but this one was not in my head. "Why are you crying?" the voice asked. "Don't you understand what's going on? There's a reason for everything that has happened in your life." This was the first time I had ever felt the Creator's presence. Eventually, two kind men heard my cries and pulled me out.

From that night on, I have always known that a force greater than myself and my small life existed in the universe. Knowing that it would accompany me into the future relieved me of any fear. I've never really known fear since, and I have felt comfortable going places where others wouldn't dare venture.

Despite my spiritual awakening, my family had little use for organized religion. As a fourth generation American Jew from an assimilated family, I'd never had a Jewish education or learned Hebrew. Grandma Rose lit candles on Friday nights but we did not observe Shabbat. We would go out to the movies in the evening or otherwise go about our business on Saturdays. My background was totally secular. Take Yom Kippur, we would gather as a family and eat on that Holy Day not so much because we were Jews but because there was nothing else to do since all the stores and restaurants in our neighborhood were closed. There was no fasting, no self-examination, no atonement. It was just a good excuse for a family get-together.

Nevertheless, I developed the spiritual side of my self long before I met Rabbi Philip Gruberger. After the incident at the construction site, I needed to understand why I could feel the Creator's constant presence, so I immersed myself in books about energy, spiritualism, reincarnation, and astrology. At a very young age I taught myself to become a psychic medium. This was a part of my life that I could feel good about. The more feminine arts of the 1950s like fashion, make-up, cooking, homemaking—the things my classmates were into—and women's magazines and homey

TV shows exalted, were lost on me. That wasn't the role I was meant to play. I was not going to be much interested in conventional norms; instead I would look more to my inner life, to feeling and having empathy for other people.

Soon things improved. When I was twelve, I had a teacher who recognized my potential and nurtured it. By high school, I'd surpassed my classmates and was placed in honors English.

When I was sixteen, I couldn't bear another disruptive move to Florida. I wanted to stay in New York to finish high school, so to support myself I took that job at Rabbi Gruberger's insurance agency and worked there for six months. In retrospect, I'm amazed at how oblivious the two of us were about what the future held in store, nonetheless at that moment we were completely unready for each other. More than that, I disliked the man, and he probably didn't have much respect for me.

At seventeen, I married a wonderful young man and quit my job at the insurance office. At that age I didn't know much about life but I appreciated the necessity to make a life for myself away from the chaos of my family. My first husband was a kind person who gave selflessly of himself, so I set about trying to create the stable home environment I'd never known. Our first child Leah was born when I was eighteen. One year later, her sister Suri arrived.

We enjoyed all the trappings of success. We lived in a big house in the Howard Beach section of Queens, near what was then Idyllwild Airport (now JFK), and my first husband bought me a brand-new Cadillac as a gift. But despite his love and his generosity, I began to feel restless and unhappy. Although all of my material needs were fulfilled, I felt strangely empty. I loved my husband as a brother and wanted to remain his friend, but we were not a spiritual match. I needed someone to challenge me, someone who would help me grow. It became clear to me that I couldn't stay in the marriage.

Although our marital bonds were loosening, I was very fond of this man. Since our wedding, I'd been working with him to help grow his company as a building contractor. Business was thriving. I enjoyed the work and didn't want to leave it, so I stayed on for a while despite my discomfort. I also didn't yet have a place to land—safely or otherwise.

I'd kept in occasional contact with Hershel Wuilliger, calling him every once in a while just to stay in touch. When I needed to help my husband find a secretary, I remembered a very competent lady who had worked at the insurance agency. I called her a few weeks after Passover in 1969 to see if she knew of anyone who could fill the position. We had a brief conversation, and just as we were about to hang up, I asked politely, "Is Mr. Gruberger still involved in the business? Do you ever see him?"

"Well, actually he doesn't live here anymore," she told me. "He moved to Israel years ago. But from time to time when he's in New York, he does pick up his mail at the office."

"Oh, nice," I said. "If you see him, please say hello for me." And I hung up without giving it another thought. As it happened, however, that same day Philip Gruberger had just flown back from Israel and walked into his office just as his secretary was hanging up the phone. She told him that I had been on the line, asking about him. He was both surprised and curious.

Not ten minutes later, my phone rang. It was my former boss. Rather than the casual, "Hi!" I'd asked her to convey, his secretary told him, "Karen called. *Call her back*," which was definitely not the message I'd left. Although I wasn't particularly thrilled to hear from him, I felt startled and strangely flustered at the sound of his voice.

"How are you?" he asked after introducing himself.

"Oh, fine," I replied. At this point, my mind was racing. Why would this man call me now, after nine years? Does he even remember who I am? Why would he care how I'm doing? Why would I want to know how or what he's doing? Unaware of his transformation, my opinion of him was still unflattering.

"So what are you up to these days?" I asked.

"I've been studying Kabbalah for the last seven years with my teacher in Israel. He passed away a few days ago, so that's why I've come home."

Now, I was intrigued and also surprised. Remembering the Philip Gruberger I had worked for, I asked him rather bluntly, "What do you know about Kabbalah?"

From my readings on reincarnation and astrology I knew that Kabbalah was the seed of all spiritual teachings, and I never would have associated this man with that mystical aspect of Judaism. It seemed so incongruent. But when he told me that he'd spent the last few years learning

Kabbalah in Israel, my ears pricked up, and we launched into a real conversation. He even confided that he had become depressed after the recent loss of his teacher. As our chat drew to a close, he invited me out to dinner at a kosher restaurant in Williamsburg that night. And I accepted.

At dinner, we could feel the connection. He was a Leo (a fire sign) and I was a Libra (an air sign). Fire and air signs go well together because Libra fans Leo's flame. How does the air sign benefit? It gains the opportunity to share and become purposeful.

The Rav may not have been thinking about astrology at dinner, yet both of us knew right then and there that we were meant for each other. Strong, persistent, perceptive, intelligent, and charming, this man was everything I wanted in a husband. He had a great capacity for love, and I could tell he genuinely cared about people. More than that, he was deeply connected to his spiritual roots, so we were matched in that way too.

Between bites of dinner, I asked him an impulsive question. "Can I make a deal with you?"

"What kind of deal?" he wanted to know.

Since he hadn't yet confided in me that his businesses were failing, I blurted, "If I come back to work for you for free, would you teach me everything you know about Kabbalah?"

Much later, my husband often spoke about how my question had shocked him—Kabbalah was not to be taught to the uninitiated, and certainly not to women. Instructing me would mean breaking with millennia of tradition. But he also described how unaffected and innocent I was in that moment. He saw me as a pure channel. Torn between these two perspectives, he couldn't answer me, not just yet. He needed to seek guidance from his teacher.

Three weeks later, we met for a life-altering conversation over breakfast at Ratner's, the one that opens this chapter. The Rav looked positively downcast. After we'd settled into our red leatherette seats, he said, "I have something to tell you."

"Well, I have something to tell you, too!" I replied excitedly.

He nodded gravely and said, "You go first."

"I had the strangest dream last night," I explained. "A man I'd never seen before approached me. When I turned to look at him, he put out his hands and held them over my head. He said something to me in a foreign language, maybe Hebrew? But I didn't understand the words. Then he turned to leave. I tried to grab his coat and ask him what he was saying but he had vanished, evaporating into thin air."

Rather than being disturbed by my peculiar dream, the Rav sat up and his face brightened. "Describe this man," he said.

The images had been quite vivid, so I could easily provide details. "He was dressed in a long black coat like yours, but he walked with a cane," I explained. "He also had a big, round felt hat on his head."

Now the Rav became flushed and animated. "This is such good news," he said. "Before going to sleep last night, I asked my teacher to come to me and assure me that it was permissible for me to teach you, a woman, Kabbalah. He never came, and so I had a heavy heart this morning because I knew I would have to call off our deal. But my teacher came to *your* dream instead. And even more importantly, when he put his hands over your head, he gave you his blessing."

The Rav's enthusiasm about the dream was contagious. And even though I was familiar with the experience of being a spiritual medium, it was still thrilling for me to have had a direct experience like this—a visitation.

* * *

A few days after our breakfast, in the middle of May, the Rav returned to Israel to visit his estranged family. He also went for the observance of Shavuot, the holiday that connects us to the revelation of the Ten Commandments or as the Rav would call them, the "Ten Utterances." Kabbalistically, this is the time when the Sefirot, "quantum packets of conscious, intelligent, energy," as the Rav would describe them, become available to us in this physical world. A cosmic connection—or a marriage, if you will—is established between the Light and the Vessel, the Creator and humankind. Two years later, the Rav and I were married just before this holiday—our worlds brought together at the same time the Light became one with its Vessel.

The Light revealed at Mount Sinai left no room for darkness anywhere on Earth. For the forty days between the time the people of Israel heard the voice of the Creator and Moses came back down the mountain, sickness and death were banished from the world. Anyone who was blemished or imperfect was made whole. Those who were blind could see; those who had lost limbs had their arms or legs restored.

Although this state of immortality was meant to be eternal, it proved to be short-lived. The Israelites grew impatient with Moses's absence. Fearing that he would never return, they consorted with an idol—a golden calf—and at that moment immortality vanished from the world.

The conduit for such a revelation does not disappear, however, its potential remains. Rav Brandwein taught the Rav that when humanity awakens its consciousness, the energy of immortality can be accessed again. The Rav said that this teaching was his first inkling that we have the capacity to live forever in a physical body. This was a subject that the Rav would return to often, and in many ways, it became the central purpose of his life and his work in the Kabbalah Centre. He would embrace it with unshakable certainty. But that came later.

The Rav left New York just prior to Shavuot to become steeped in this holiday of revelation, Light, and immortality in Jerusalem. Was this a foreshadowing of our two worlds coming together? Not long after that, the Rav agreed to teach Kabbalah to me. Was this the seed level of the Light of Kabbalah becoming fully revealed into this world and creating an awareness of this knowledge of immortality? Today, people can access this information in classes at the Centre, and also from the Rav's many books including Immortality: The Inevitablity of Eternal Life and Nano: The Technology of Mind over Matter. Did this all grow from the moment the universe conspired to bring us together?

Perhaps being imbued with the energy of Shavuot, this supported the Rav in his decision to teach me, the first woman ever to study Kabbalah in public. Maybe he felt that now was the right time, since Shavuot corresponds with the time that the Vessel is ready.

I can only imagine what went through the Rav's mind during that time. He had been raised in a closed, rigid system. Kabbalah was the innermost sanctum. For centuries, it had only been studied by a tiny and exclusive group of men. It was protected and held close by some of the greatest sages of all time. And here I was, twenty-something, very secular, an uninitiated soon-to-be divorcée illiterate in Hebrew, asking to be admitted into this sacred space.

Looking back on the Rav's process, his internal struggle boggles the mind. *Should I teach Karen or shouldn't I? Should I violate the code of conduct or shouldn't I? I have my teacher's blessing, but still!* To decide to share a secret that he held with such awe and reverence, to break with centuries of tradition, what did that mean to him? The Rav was not the kind of person to take this lightly. The opposite was true, in fact. Although he was capable of pioneering great change, as demonstrated by his ability to bring together religious and political worlds, he deeply respected the institutions he served and represented. What strength, conviction, and love this decision must have required.

Yet decide he did. While he was in Israel for those few weeks, he sent me the most magnificent letters. In one ten-page missive he wrote about the steps I would need to go through in order to learn Kabbalah. He wrote to me about birth and rebirth. He promised to be my guide, to help me in a process he had previously considered impossible. I was to be his first student. I had believed that I could never be a part of Kabbalah but now this was becoming a reality for both of us.

Similarly, the letters the Rav had received from his first soul mate, Rav Brandwein, were indispensable to him in advancing his learning and serving as an expression of love and support when the Rav had to be in New York. Now that these roles had shifted and the Rav had become the teacher and I his student, his letters served the same purpose—igniting my desire to learn and preparing me for the transmission of this wisdom. They echoed the teacher-student bond the Rav had felt for Rav Brandwein, and now, in turn, I felt blessed to love—and be loved—so greatly.

* * *

The Rav returned to the United States for a few months and answered all my questions about religion and traditional practices—subjects I knew almost nothing about. As a spiritual medium I had questions of my own for the powers that be. I asked the universe whether the Rav was "the one." If so, I promised to go through hell and high water to be with him. "But if not," I said out loud, "do me a favor and take him away."

The answer consistently came back, "Yes, you have to marry him." This confirmed my sense that we were both part of the same soul, in the same line of souls. I knew this marriage was something we had to do, however difficult it might be. Already I realized this wasn't going to be a typical tale of a man and a woman who fall in love, get married, and open a business together like my first marriage. That was not going to be our life.

I hadn't yet learned that the perfect kabbalistic soul mate bond is not made of two entities but rather of three—including the Light of the Creator. Mutual desire for the Light is the glue of this connection. The Rav's purpose had become mine, and we had merged in this way even before we got married. I didn't have the language or the perspective to see this at that time; I only sensed that our future marriage would always involve some form of service.

For now, though, we couldn't reside together, since there was the matter of our prior marriages to resolve. I was still living in the house in Howard Beach with my estranged husband. And the sexual revolution notwithstanding, the Rav and I were not physically intimate, for this would have violated the strict Orthodox rules governing that kind of behavior. We had to divorce our first spouses first and marry each other—no easy task, as you'll soon see.

In the meantime, the Rav and I decided that if we wanted to create the foundation for a strong marriage, we needed to make some spiritual preparations. People believe that I changed because he asked me to but I would never have done so had I not been convinced that this was the only way our marriage could thrive. I formally separated from my estranged husband and moved with our girls to a small apartment on Avenue N in Brooklyn, part of a religious neighborhood where we could acclimate to this very different way of being. Together with my two girls, I started to observe Shabbat and keep kosher. They put away their blue jeans and summer dresses in favor of modest blouses and skirts so long they nearly brushed the sidewalks. What a difficult time this was, for them and for me.

My estranged husband didn't take my decision to move out all that well and promised to cut me off if I left him. He took back my fancy car, and suddenly I found myself struggling financially. But I had decided that this man, the Rav, and what he had to offer—a life studying and living Kabbalah—was what I really wanted. So I traded the house, the car, and the alimony payments for a tiny apartment for me and the girls in Brooklyn and a welfare check.

My mother couldn't believe it. "How do you decide to give away the good life you have? You're crazy! What can this man give you? What can he offer? He's too old for you. And so religious!"

But it didn't feel crazy to me at all. It felt just right.

* * *

I once heard a beautiful story that gave me a new perspective on what it means to be soul mates. Every day, a man journeyed to a well to fill his two buckets of water. One was sound, but the other had a small crack in it. After filling his buckets, he made the long trek home. By the time he arrived, one bucket remained full of water, and not surprisingly the cracked bucket was only half full. He kept this up for years and years, until one night he had a dream.

In his sleep the damaged bucket came to him and said, "I feel so bad that after so much time you're still carrying me. I know that you don't want to throw me away but I only carry half as much water as I should, and you have to make nearly the same effort to bring me back home as you would if I were perfect and full."

The man replied, "Did you notice on our way home, there are so many spectacular flowers on the left side of our path? Well, you water those flowers with your slow trickle every day. My path has been made beautiful by these flowers; they give me such joy! This is why it's so important that you have that crack."

Like the imperfect bucket, each one of us has a flaw; we might be too needy, too well protected, or even too self-assured. Yet that imperfection helps bring energy to the people around us. In fact, I believe that a crack is only a flaw if we choose to perceive it that way. The man in the story had a wonderful way of seeing the perfection in the crack, for this made it possible to water the flowers that beautified his way.

The Rav knew that my flaw was being a pleaser. I used to get myself into messes because I couldn't set limits. I divided myself into too many pieces. I would say, "Sure,

I can do that," and then try to fit my new commitment into an impossibly complex schedule. It's not that I was eager to engage in so many activities; I just had a hard time saying no. I didn't want anyone to dislike me, and I was afraid they would if I stood up for myself.

But being with the Rav and learning Kabbalah taught me that it was time to start setting priorities. I had reached a place where I understood that I had to define for myself what was important and not be guided by my inner eight-year-old, that needy little girl who craved attention and affection. This was my opponent, which was perfectly understandable given my childhood. Also, as a Libra I tend to be very open, so setting boundaries felt inflexible, which went against my nature.

The Rav, being a Leo, was my polar opposite. He was always fixed in his truths and clear about parameters, all of which I found very attractive. He had been the baby in the family, the favorite son. He had graduated from rabbinical training, hobnobbed with famous politicians, and had been tremendously successful in business. He fulfilled, and then exceeded, all of his parents' aspirations. So in a way, the crack in his bucket was just the opposite of mine—he was utterly self-contained. But that's how the soul mate union works. We fill in for each other's deficits and contribute new value. My flexibility balanced his focus. His strength fortified my sensitivity. And together we took my favorite road, the one less travelled, and made it something accepted that was for everyone.

This was so important spiritually. Women are endowed with a special responsibility to help men manifest their purpose in the world, their *tikkun*. Think of the sun and the moon. The sun represents male energy, referred to as Zeir Anpin (the six Sefirot that deliver the Light to this physical world). The moon represents female energy, Malchut, the level of kingdom, the dimension of materialization, the force of receiving, the Vessel. Male and female complement each other. The moon enhances the sun's ability to shine, even during the night. The beautiful part of this dynamic is that the sun never sees the dark side of the moon since it is always shining in the sun's presence.

Sun and moon, we would soon make our way in the universe together, but then the unimaginable happened.

While Rivka and the children were still in Jerusalem and the Rav and I were still sorting things out about our future lives, the Rav got the terrible news that his youngest daughter, three-year-old Miriam Esther, had developed cancer. Doctors in Israel believed the child had lymphoma. In those years the medical system in Israel was not yet state of the art, so I said to the Rav, "Bring her to the States. I know plenty of doctors who can help. Let's treat her here."

With her father's help, Rivka soon moved the family back to New York. She brought Miriam Esther to a hospital in Brooklyn, where my friend was the chairman of the department of head and neck surgery. There, the little girl was properly diagnosed with leukemia, which today is a relatively curable diagnosis, but not back then. She was treated in the hospital for three months but then, tragically, she died.

When this happened, the Rav's whole world split apart, not only from the pain and devastation of his child's death but also because he finally communicated to Rivka that their separation was final. The marriage was over.

"I can't live with you anymore," he told her, and he asked her for a legal and a religious divorce.

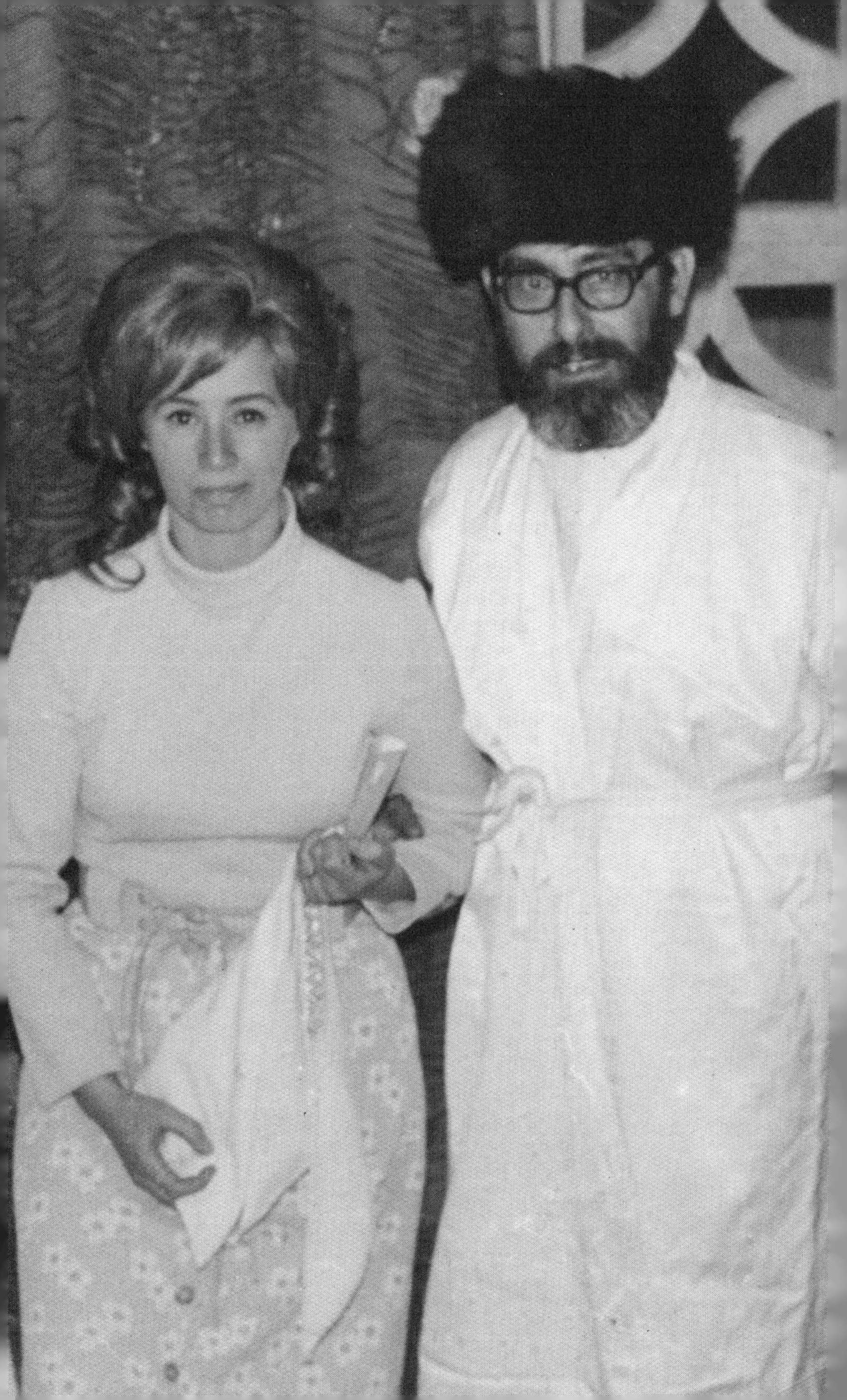

CHAPTER 5:

ALL HELL BREAKS LOOSE

When Rivka and her family came to the United States for Miriam Esther's diagnosis and treatment, this created an opening that would settle whether or not the Rav and I would have a life together. The Rav told me that his marriage had been arranged—it was a *shidduch*. He had married Rivka because she was a direct descendent of the House of David, and he and his parents wanted his children to share that lineage. But there was no special bond between husband and wife.

I can't speak for Rivka, and she has left this world (may her soul rest in peace). What I can say is that within the Orthodox community at that time, women had no real voice. For years, Rivka had remained in New York and did not openly object even when her husband decided to move to Israel and live close by his teacher. The Rav told me that Rivka decided to move to Jerusalem with their children because she believed it would be less expensive and because the family would have more access to him. She was there for about a year before Rav Brandwein died and the Rav returned to the United States, leaving her one more time.

Although they kept getting separated, Rivka was an unwilling party to this arrangement. And now I was in the picture. Rivka's arrival in Brooklyn and her sudden awareness of my connection to her estranged husband started what I think of as a religious war, with me and the Rav on one side and the American branch of the Brandwein family and the New York Orthodox community on the other. For the two years between 1969 and 1971, the opposition tried anything and everything to separate us.

Of course, they were completely unaware of the deep spiritual connection between us. They saw only a rabbi leaving his family for a much younger woman—and a non-religious one at that. As difficult as this was for us, with hindsight we were able to see how much this opposition contributed to our growth. The Rav used to say about opposites: "If an idea is not accepted by a group, then this idea is probably very significant." Of course this would also apply to our work later of spreading the wisdom of Kabbalah. In the end, however, the strategy of antagonism backfired on our challengers. It only served to draw the Rav closer to me, confirming our belief that this was truly a connection between soul mates.

Our situation reminded the Rav of the story of Jacob, Leah, and Rachel. He used to say that before he studied Kabbalah that story always confused him. Rachel had been the love of Jacob's life, yet after seven years of working for her father, Jacob was tricked into marrying Rachel's sister, Leah. He had to work seven more years to win Rachel, but after he finally married her, she died. He lost her, he had her, and then he lost her again. "What's the point of this story?" the Rav used to wonder.

The Zohar provided some answers, and he loved the story once he understood its spiritual significance. Rachel represented this physical world, or the lower, material level: Malchut. After Jacob struggled with the angel of negativity and won, he raised his consciousness and became a being of a higher level; to reflect this transformation the angel changed his name from Jacob to Israel. At that point, he needed a wife who suited his elevated being. Leah was Binah—of the upper level, as reflected in her eyes, which were described as being like a veil. Her essence was less physical and more ethereal. So Jacob had two soul mate marriages: Rachel was his soul mate before his transformation; Leah became his soul mate later, when he elevated to Israel, and he lived out the rest of his days with her.

The lesson for the Rav in this was that when we're ready, we get the mate that suits us. In today's world this shift of consciousness requires divorce. This notion is reinforced in the Zohar, which explains that the matter of divorce is cosmically synchronized with the *tikkun* process of reincarnation and soul mates. If the first union is not a soul marriage (and few are, explained Rav Shimon), a couple may divorce to allow one spouse or the other (or both) to unite with their soul mate in a second marriage to bring forth Light.

For many people, however, divorce is still considered a source of shame, and it can trigger terrible strife within families. Nevertheless, divorce provides people who possess the free will and self-determination to end a marriage with a way to satisfy the *tikkun* process. Of course, this doesn't mean that all men should divorce their wives or vice versa! However divorce and remarriage can play an active role in the elevation of a soul's purpose.

In the Zohar, Rav Shimon wrote that the spiritually elevated soul reaches into its deepest yearnings to connect to its soul mate. He used the love affair between David and Batsheva to explain how this works.

> *When David committed his great sin in taking Batsheva, he thought that it would leave its mark forever. But the message came to him, "The Lord hath put away thy sin, thou shalt not die;" i.e. the stain has been removed. Rav Aba put this question to Rav Shimon: "Since we have been taught that Batsheva was destined for King David from the day of the Creation, how come the Lord first gave her to Uriah the Hittite?" Rav Shimon replied: "Such is the way of the Lord; although a woman is destined for a certain man, the Creator first allows her to be the wife of another man until the time of the soul mate arrives (he has elevated himself spiritually)."*

Appreciating the kabbalistic principles of reincarnation helps prepare individuals for their long marriage adventure, especially when divorce is involved. My husband used to explain that the kinds of bitter struggles that can accompany the unsettling effects of divorce (such as the ones we'd experienced) need not emerge. And the knowledge of the *tikkun* process and the reincarnation principle can help people weather the storms that may rage during a divorce.

It was Kabbalah that helped the Rav and I to stay the course during our most difficult times together. After all, if it wasn't to share the energy of the Light through Kabbalah, why would we be together in the first place? We were joined to create a conduit for this wisdom. Otherwise, the critics would have been right. Our marriage didn't make any sense, nor did it stand a chance! From that spiritual perspective, however, it did and we did, for the more than four decades we were husband and wife.

Rav Isaac Luria (the Ari) wrote in Gate of Reincarnations that bringing together a soul mate marriage is more difficult than the *Kri'at Yam Suf,* (Splitting of the Red Sea). Even though freedom may have been joyful for the Israelites, others had to perish to make it possible. The Creator said to the Israelites, "Why are you celebrating when my children [the Egyptians] are dying?" It pains the Creator when soul mates get together in situations when someone else is likely to get hurt.

How can you tell if you're looking at a soul mate marriage? The Ari said that when everything around you is chaotic and crazy, when everyone gives you a hard time because they're opposed to the marriage, yet internally you experience peace and harmony, this is the sign of a soul mate connection. This was clearly the case with the Rav and his teacher, Rav Brandwein, and later with my teacher, the Rav, and me.

There were so many levels to the chaos. First of all, before an Orthodox person can remarry, he or she needs not just a civil divorce but also a spiritual divorce called a *Get* from the first spouse. The latter unties the souls bound together by the marriage ceremony so there will be no residue of the energetic attachment. In the best of circumstances, the separating husband and wife readily grant this to each other. In the worst-case scenario, one spouse or the other can withhold the *Get*, preventing their former partner from moving on with his or her life and becoming tied on a soul level with someone else. A woman without a *Get* can never remarry, and Jewish law also proclaims that a woman may not be divorced against her will.

There was no problem in my own case. My first husband was unhappy but cooperative. We divorced legally on January 12, 1970 and later that year I received a *Get* from him written by Rabbi Moses Feinstein, an authority in religious law. So, although the dissolution of my first marriage was painful, my path to marry the Rav was now clear of obstacles. But for the Rav, the road was much more difficult. He succeeded in filing for a civil divorce, but when he asked for his soul's freedom as a religious person, Rivka denied him a *Get*.

There are complex ways around this for a man, which I'll explain in a bit, and the Rav eventually put these extreme measures into effect. However, Rivka's refusal was a source of anguish for quite some time. Without the

Get, we could not marry. To be unable to free oneself from a destructive relationship, my husband wrote years later in Wheels of a Soul, can be "devastating and psychologically paralyzing, and ultimately spiritually demoralizing." He most certainly was writing from his own experience.

A torrent of animosity was directed toward us as a couple that had nothing to do with the Rav wanting to teach Kabbalah. The religious community disliked me for many reasons, not the least of which was the fact that Rivka, because of her lineage, was related to most of the prominent rabbis in the world. She felt that the Rav should stay married to her, even if they no longer lived together. The opinions of the others were less generous. To some, I was the younger woman who stole him from his community and his family. Rumors circulated that the Rav was going to marry a *shiksa*—a gentile woman—either because they believed I wasn't Jewish or because they didn't consider me Jewish enough since I hadn't been raised in the ultra-Orthodox tradition. Some gossiped, *"Oh, he's marrying his secretary,"* as if we'd had some torrid affair when I was working at his office at the age of sixteen, which was absurd.

Some said that I was a gold-digger, which was even more ridiculous; although in fairness the Orthodox community didn't know that the Rav's businesses were in a state of collapse. Perhaps the grand rabbis believed that if the Rav married me they would lose the power and influence he had wielded on their behalf with the city government. Whatever the reasons, the religious community reacted so vehemently that one day after we were married, the Rav's name was expunged from the Yeshiva building where it had been listed in acknowledgment of his generosity.

Actually, there was great irony in this. Kabbalistically, sharing and generosity practiced in private not only reveals more Light but ultimately creates a greater connection to the spiritual realm. Anonymous giving is the most meaningful form of *tzedakah* (charity).

Nevertheless, this was one of many examples of the righteous indignation directed toward the Rav by the ultra-Orthodox community. Rabbis sent messengers demanding that he reconsider his decision to divorce and remarry but he refused to back down. This was a classic example of his legendary clarity and certainty. From the moment we'd met that second time, I was always the most important person in his life, and he would have done anything for me. Moreover, he was committed to the meaning of our relationship and to the work we came into this world to do—to reveal the wisdom of Kabbalah.

More painful than public censure was the Rav's estrangement from his children. Rivka kept them away from him. He had little contact with his three-year-old daughter, Miriam Esther, as she lay dying—the Brandweins barred him from visiting her in the hospital. The family's attitude was, "*You see what you're doing? If you'd just stayed with Rivka, this never would have happened.*" After Miriam Esther passed, she was buried on the same mountain as Rav Ashlag and Rav Brandwein; the Rav told me that he was comforted by the sight of Rav Ashlag's grave down the slope.

But there was still more pain to come. After the proper amount of time had passed, the family refused to put a headstone on the child's grave. They left this to the Rav, having learned by this time that he was broke. So he had to scrape together pennies, beg and borrow wherever he could to pay for the headstone. Not only was he grieving for his baby, but they used his child's death to shame and hurt him further.

The Rav did leave his wife and eight children, which was certainly painful for all concerned. But while he was divorcing Rivka, he never abandoned his children. On the contrary, he made every effort to have a relationship with them. If they were willing to see him, he was always there. Ten years later, the Rav's youngest son, Naftali, would live with us; we rejoiced in this reunion and welcomed Naftali with all our hearts.

During these dark times, I could see that the Rav was doing everything in his power to maintain a connection with his family but this was nearly impossible. He said to his children, "I know you don't appreciate my choices, but we can still have a relationship, can't we?"

To this, one of his daughters replied, "If you go with this woman, we will never speak to you again. We don't want anything to do with you."

After the divorce proceedings, he was only allowed to see his children during supervised visits. The family changed the children's last names to Rivka's maiden name, Brandwein.

When someone marries outside the Orthodox community, the family sits shiva for them and mourns them as if they've died. The Brandweins began treating the Rav the same way. You can't imagine how hard this was for him. There is no greater anguish for a parent than to lose a child, and the Rav had already lost one to cancer. Now he was losing his connection to the rest. Along with his teacher's passing, this was one of the most devastatingly painful times in his life. Later, the Rav said that he was being prepared for the role of helping people; having lived through so much pain himself, he could be more available for people when they suffered trials of their own.

Eventually, one of the grand ultra-Orthodox rabbis in Brooklyn, Rabbi Chabin, helped the Rav find some peace with this situation. He asked the Rav, *"If they don't want to see you, which they're showing through their actions, why see them?"* He encouraged my husband to move on. This was unbearably sad but there seemed no other way.

* * *

In the middle of this tumult, we decided to marry. In Kabbalah we teach that anytime something big is going to happen, there will be obstacles—and there were, in spades. But Light is concealed inside a challenge, and it's our job to unwrap and reveal it from the darkness. Although the Rav and Rivka had divorced legally, she still would not give him a religious divorce, a *Get*. However, there are instances in which a man can divorce and remarry even if his estranged wife disputes the break-up. In certain extreme cases when a wife refuses to divorce her husband for an extended period of time, the Jewish court or Beit Din can step in and permit a religious divorce and remarriage, but only after one hundred rabbis agree to issue an exemption of the strict law. This is no small task. The signed document they produce is called a *Heter Me'ah Rabbanim*.

Rav Brandwein's firstborn son, Moishe Chaim, turned the tide for us on this issue. Hearing of our plight, he told my husband, "I'm going to help you to get married." This was astonishing because Moishe Chaim was Rivka's first cousin. But true to his word, he arranged everything. The Rav, in his characteristically direct way, asked Moishe Chaim, "Why are you doing all this for us?"

It turns out that once again Rav Brandwein played a key role in our lives. Moishe Chaim reported a recurring dream in which his father had come to him saying, "You have to make this happen." So he arranged for the *Heter Me'ah Rabbanim*, and it was in place for our religious ceremony.

The Rav and I were married just two years after we'd reconnected, right before Shavuot on May 25, 1971 in East Jerusalem at the Commodore Hotel, a modest, family-run establishment at the foot of the Mount of Olives and just steps from the Temple Mount. A quorum of ten men (*minyan*), who were strangers to us witnessed the ceremony, which was performed by Rabbi Avraham Mordechai Horowitz, the head of the Beit Din that Rav Brandwein had established years earlier. No one else attended—not even my children, who we'd left with some close friends in Brooklyn. There were no flowers, no fancy dress, no trappings of a festive wedding—but that didn't matter to us.

The exchange of vows was followed by a small meal, and then the Rav and I walked down to the Kotel, the Western Wall. Ordinarily men and women are separated at the Wall—each gender has its own section. But when we told the guard, "We just got married today!" he let us go in and dance together, just the two of us. We were thrilled to be able to enjoy our wedding dance at the Western Wall. We certainly looked like the Odd Couple, me with my relatively short skirt and the Rav dressed in his long coat and *spudick*, the fur hat customary on festive occasions.

We remained in Israel three days. Normally, after a wedding, seven blessings—the sheva brachot—are repeated for seven days but for a second marriage, these blessings are repeated for only three days. During this time, we traveled to Meron in northern Israel and said the blessing of the *sheva brachot* at the grave of Rav Shimon Bar Yochai. Once again I was allowed into the men's section for this blessing ceremony. I later learned how unique this was; in all of my years returning to these special places, I have never once witnessed a woman dancing on the men's side of the Kotel or praying in the men's section near Rav Shimon's grave. Perhaps it was Divine intervention.

The third night we returned to Jerusalem and performed the sheva brachot at Rav Brandwein's small place of study in the Old City. It was in the *shtibl* (little room for prayer) that the Histadrut had given him in 1967 after the Six-Day War—the building where he and the Rav learned together and they experienced Shabbat together. This space held many memories and much meaning for the Rav, and together we felt Rav Brandwein's presence there.

After three days it was back to Brooklyn, the girls, and our new life together.

* * *

Our honeymoon ended quickly! Even though we were now officially divorced and married religiously, the road ahead would be difficult. (Our civil marriage took place several months later on July 19, 1971 at a courthouse in Greenwich, Connecticut.) Like my mother, many people tut-tutted. *"You're a young girl marrying an older man. This relationship won't work."* Even the Rav's closest friend during those years, Bernie Lander, a social scientist, leader in the Jewish community, and founder of Touro College said to us, "Karen, what are you doing? You guys could never be a good match."

I responded, "I didn't marry him for the usual reasons. I married him because I was able to see a potential to do something far greater with our lives. I see in him a higher purpose. But Bernie, why are you saying this?"

He repeated, "Because he's too religious for you. You've never lived that kind of life, and it's never going to work."

I smiled, and the Rav smiled. And guess what? It worked.

However, in some ways, Bernie was right. The Rav and I were soul mates but that didn't mean we didn't struggle. We were parts of the same soul, yes, but we came from "across the sea." In many ways those were the best years of our lives but I won't pretend that they were easy. The places where we compensated for each other's cracks were also the places where we had the most conflict. We argued a lot.

* * *

God bless the Rav's soul, of course he wanted us to live in a strictly religious neighborhood, which we did. But for me, it was like trying to fit a square peg into a round hole. Our first years together were not simple, and the problems didn't just arise from the community. There were family issues we needed to settle, especially between us and with my two girls. We had told them that we were going to Israel for a few days, but we never explained that we were planning to get married. When we came back to New York as husband and wife the two of us were thrilled, however, the two of them were quite surprised—shocked is a better word. Looking back on it, we could have handled that better.

Also, after returning from Israel, we lived like displaced people. By this point the Rav had lost all of the fortune he had amassed years earlier. Nor could he continue working with his old partner, Hershel Wuilliger, since Hershel was Rivka's sister's husband. So he went to work for someone else, but any money he made went first to his family, for the kids. We had nada, absolutely nothing.

This formerly wealthy man had to borrow $25 so we could buy groceries to make a Shabbat meal. And our accommodations were challenging, to say the least. When my two girls moved out of their father's house and in with me, they went from living in a beautiful home and having every material possession they could dream of to a tiny unfurnished apartment on Avenue N with mattresses on the floor. And now the Rav had moved in with us.

Then there was the religious issue. Suri and Leah had never learned anything about Judaism except the fact that they were born into it. Now, in the heart of ultra-Orthodox religious life in Brooklyn, it felt like they had been relocated to a different planet. We enrolled them in a Yeshiva so they could acclimate. But the transition from a public education to a demanding religious school was unsettling, to say the least. They were required to wear different clothing and live by new strict rules. Moreover, they needed to speak and read in Yiddish, a language they had never heard, much less learned! Leah had to repeat the first grade because she couldn't quickly master Jewish studies. Since Orthodox children had been immersed in Judaism from birth, this requirement felt arbitrary and unfair.

To make matters more difficult, although the Rav was very different from the man I'd first met, he still hadn't developed the sensitivity to appreciate how alien the Orthodox lifestyle was to us. So there were arguments about Shabbat, and the rules for keeping kosher, and visits with the girls' father and our respective families.

Whereas the Rav was very strict about observing all of the kosher precepts to the letter, my former husband had been as likely to eat a bacon cheeseburger on Yom Kippur as not. My children would get into trouble with the Rav after a visit to their non-religious dad if they had eaten something at his house that wasn't kosher. The Rav was tough on the girls, believing it was good for them. The Rav used to tell them, "You know how you get a diamond from coal? You put a lot of pressure on it."

Both girls used to sit on the floor in the apartment in Brooklyn, stuffing letters requesting donations into envelopes. This was their volunteer work, he would say, their acts of sharing. It wasn't easy for my children, and I felt for them. It's difficult to be suddenly plunged into a totally new way of living and to have no choice in the matter. It was a rough transition for them.

Meanwhile the Rav and I struggled to provide them with a good example. The two of us fought, and then fought some more. Right after we got married, the Rav discarded all of my books on astrology and spirituality—he threw them out. I couldn't believe it! He went crazy over things that seemed like nonsense to me. Once, he went to the *mikvah*—the ritual spiritual purification bath—to cleanse himself before the Sabbath. Suri accidentally brushed against his hand after this ritual, and he hit the roof!

We argued over a television set. We didn't have one in the apartment, so I brought a small one home. He blocked the doorway and pushed it out of our apartment as if it was a dead cat. When I ran into the hallway to retrieve it, he closed the door behind me. So I took the TV and left him in the apartment with my daughters.

When I finally called him later that evening, he asked, "You're leaving me? Because of a TV? It's a stupidity!"

"That's right," I retorted. "It is a stupidity."

Late that night I came home with the TV. And it stayed.

It takes two to argue. For my part, I got so fed up with his religiosity that one day I took that big, black fur hat off his head and flung it right out the window! I said to him, "Let's get something clear. I changed my life to be with you. I joined your world but you've got to come into mine a little too. I can't live under such strict rules." At another point, I remember saying to him, "Well, you know who I am, and my life is not your life. I need time to find my way," and I did. But I had to find it on my own, and that took about two years.

The Rav could be stubborn but he was also capable of great love. Fortunately, I wasn't cowed by his assertiveness. I openly disagreed with him in ways few people in his life ever did. Eventually, my girls learned to love him very much. As my daughter Leah put it, "The Rav was very tough, strong, and determined in many ways but then I would see his soft side. I saw it in the little things, whether with adults, children, or animals. He had loving, caring compassion for everything and everyone."

Because of his open heart, the Rav and I never gave up on our commitment to each other. Despite all the wrangling, we could not bear to be without each other. It was a paradox. Although merging our two worlds was difficult, our shared desire to create something bigger than ourselves prevailed. In fact, it was our differences that would eventually make it possible for us to create a Kabbalah Centre accessible to everyone.

* * *

Another factor that made our lives bearable during those times was our ability to have fun together. The Rav had his surprising dimensions. His serious demeanor and formal attire masked a silly sense of humor, and he made me laugh all the time. My mother had a cat named Ginger. One day, when the Rav and I were by ourselves in her duplex, he called, "Ginger!" When she jumped up and started to run, he said, "Oh, this looks like fun." So he chased the cat around the house. I was laughing so hard I could hardly breathe. "Stop already!" I told him between giggles. "Leave Ginger alone!"

Ginger clearly enjoyed the moment as much as he did. However, every time he walked into my mother's house, Ginger gave him a curious look, as if she was wondering what this crazy man was going to do next. He and I would glance at each other and burst out laughing all over again.

Another time I was in the kitchen in our small Brooklyn apartment when the Rav squirted me with a seltzer bottle. So I picked up another seltzer bottle and squirted him back. We ran around our apartment spraying each other like two kids playing with water pistols in the park. Once, after a major snowfall, we were wrestling and he threw me into a snowbank. I pretended I couldn't get up, and when he leaned over to help me, I tripped him and pulled him into the snow with me. We behaved like children, which was great fun. And we needed every bit of that comic relief because day-by-day, our situation within the community grew darker.

* * *

Even after our marriage was a done deal, the harassment continued. It wasn't just the Brandweins. The Rav's family was even worse. They began to physically harass us, and the abuse intensified over time. They threw rocks at the windows of our apartment at all hours of the day and night. They ordered pizzas delivered to the house at 2 or 3 o'clock in the morning, waking all of us.

Since we were all living in the same neighborhood, I couldn't simply avoid those who wished us ill. One day, I passed one of Rivka's relatives on the street, who looked away muttering something nasty. I was so tired of the abuse that something inside me snapped. I started running down the street after her, screaming "Why don't you look me in the eye and tell me those things? You want to say something? I'm here. Look at me." But she just kept on walking.

One day, the Rav's sister-in-law came after me on the street. She smacked me in the head with a baseball bat and knocked me to the pavement. I blacked out, suffered a concussion, and had to be hospitalized. When the Rav and I went to the police to report the incident, the detective said, "If you charge this woman with assault with a deadly weapon—which is well within your rights—I'll have to arrest her, and she will need to stay in jail at least overnight while the judge sets bail. If this goes to trial, she could be sentenced to five years in prison."

The Rav and I looked at each other. I shrugged and said, "Forget it. I don't want to do that." I couldn't stomach putting the woman in prison, no matter how hateful she was being. We dropped the charges.

Although that attack was terrible, it also had a positive effect. It helped us realize that we couldn't continue to live in that neighborhood. Life had become impossible for us there. So first we took off to the Five Towns area, a group of villages in Nassau County on the South Shore of Long Island close to Queens where there was an Orthodox community. But then we decided to hell with it! We're not going to stay in New York. Late in the summer of 1971, we picked up and moved to Israel with the girls, leaving everything behind but our meager savings.

We didn't know where we were going to live or how we were going to pay the bills. None of us spoke Hebrew. The Rav was fluent in what they call *Lashon Kodesh*, the language of the Bible, but he had conversed with Rav Brandwein in Yiddish, and he had never learned Modern Hebrew. Thanks to my secular upbringing, I had had no Hebrew at all, and neither did my girls. Then I discovered that I was pregnant.

This is how we began the next stage of our lives—in poverty, with chaos and animosity swirling all around us. With naysayers and attackers. With a titanic clash of values and lifestyles. But that was not how we ended up. We had nothing, yet there was magic between the two of us. We had both been well off and we gave it all up, leaving our old lives behind to build something new because we believed in it with all of our hearts.

It was a decision we would never have reason to regret.

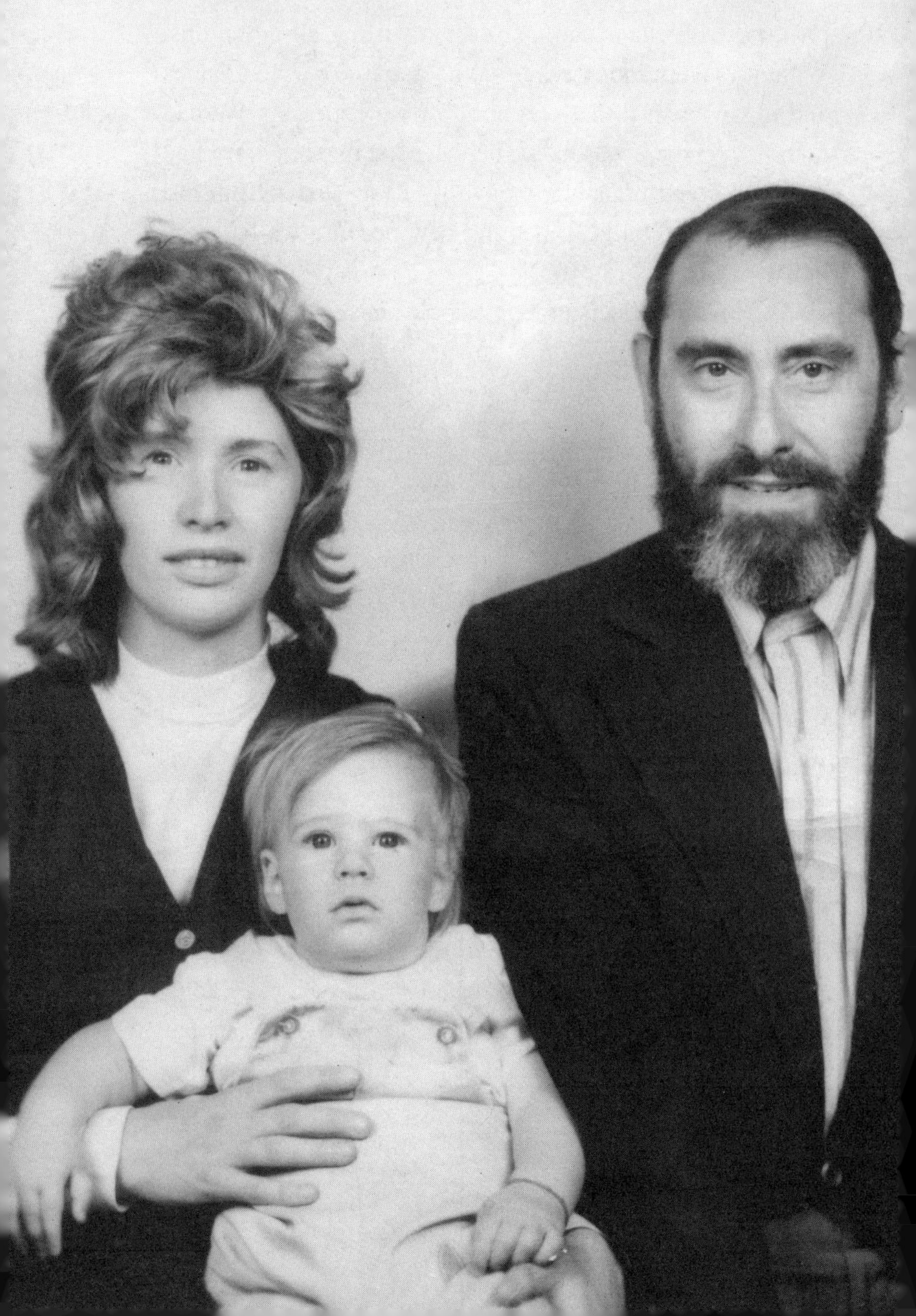

CHAPTER 6:

THE SEED OF A NEW BEGINNING

In the early fall of 1971, we moved to Israel. We had no language. No family. No friends. No money. No *nada*. It was the Rav and me against the world, absolutely the Rav and me against the world.

When our plane landed at Lod Airport near Tel Aviv, some strangers came over to greet our little family of four—Leah, Suri, the Rav and I. They asked us, "What are you doing here?"

"We're making *aliyah*," the Rav explained. "We're immigrating to Israel."

One of these strangers, an older gentleman, turned to the Rav, who was easily identifiable as religious because of his garb, and asked, "Do you know anybody here?"

When my husband indicated that he didn't, Rabbi Kahana offered his assistance. He had been second in command at the Misrad HaDatot, the Israeli Ministry of Religious Affairs, and he said to us, "If you need help, please call me." It was amazing. He knew nothing about us—not about the *Get* or our marriage, or the Rav's alienated children, or the violence, or the baby on the way—except that we were making *aliyah* and that we had little in the way of resources or contacts. That was all he needed to know.

With gratitude in our hearts, we gathered our belongings and took a taxi to a dingy hotel in Jerusalem. After a few days, having nothing to lose, the Rav decided to call the phone number Dr. Kahana had given us. True to his word, he found a place on Mt. Zion where the Rav could teach every night so we would have a little income. It was like a nightclub with Israeli singers, although there's really nothing comparable to it in the United States. Tourists would come in, pay a cover charge, order a bottle of wine and a light meal, and be entertained.

The Rav's role at the club was to introduce patrons to biblical stories. He would talk about King David, how he'd set his harp in such a way that the wind would hit certain strings to wake him at midnight so the king could arise to write the Psalms. I accompanied my husband from time to time, and it was lovely. The Rav did this for maybe six months, and then began teaching philosophy of religion part-time at Jerusalem University. Dr. Kahana was also able to help us secure a small government stipend because the Rav was engaged in religious activities. Eventually, we had enough money to rent a small, fourth floor walk-up apartment on the other side of the city.

Between his work at the university and at the nightclub, and the support we received, we were able to sustain our little family for a few years as the Rav became the man who would bring Kabbalah to the larger world. It wasn't easy for the Rav to give up his old life and start from scratch.

During those first months we were demoralized, which is especially hard on a Leo, whose most prominent feature is his splendor. For the Rav, this time of soul-searching was accompanied by a lack of clarity that was uncharacteristic for him. You could say it was a time of darkness. Nevertheless, he accepted it because of his love for me and because, despite the obstacles, he was sure he was on the right road.

* * *

The Study of the Ten Luminous Emanations describes the process that lead to the Creation of this physical world and how we can navigate through it. The book provides a wonderful framework for understanding the next steps in the Rav's personal journey. As we ascend from dimension to dimension, climbing the Tree of Life from the lowest level in the material world up through the higher levels of consciousness—the Ten Sefirot—we encounter spiritual ladders. When we reach the top rung of one ladder we need to reach over to the bottom of the next, and in between there's a gap. Here, in this void, we encounter what feels like darkness: the unknown. Here we must exercise our free will and choose whether or not to continue the journey.

This requires a leap of faith. And once we catch that first rung of the next ladder, we have to cope with the discouraging feeling that we're starting again at the bottom. This is the process of growth we go through any time we elevate from one level to the next. It's like the high school senior who feels she's the master of her world until she enters college and must cope with the confusion and anxiety of starting off a lowly freshman.

This was the story of the Rav's journcy. Every time he reached the top rung of one level, he found himself in a state of questioning so as to find the way forward. Although it often felt like darkness, this space gave him room to evolve. Each time we go to this place, we're being called upon to choose is this what you really want?

As grim as our situation seemed, it was also a wonderful opportunity for us to grow as a couple and a family. Soon our first son Yehuda was born, and then a year later, Michael. We moved into a tiny apartment on Jabotinsky Street, where we lived for two years before we moved to Bar Kochba Street in an area known as French Hill. This neighborhood was populated by retired rabbis and Holocaust survivors who were not ultra-Orthodox, but still *shomer Shabbat*—observant of the Sabbath. Located in the northeast corner of Jerusalem, the area was named for a British general, John French, who garrisoned there in the late nineteenth century.

One of our common daily walks took us to the *mikvah* on Shabbat and other holidays. Then we would walk from the *mikvah* south to the Western Wall—about five kilometers—to pray. It was magical.

Many Israeli Arabs lived in our neighborhood too, and some became our friends. In those days it was unusual for a Jewish family to become close to Palestinians. These friends invited us to accompany them to the mountains of Jericho and the city of Jenin on the West Bank, which were among the most volatile areas in the region, but they vouched for us. We would even shop together in the markets of Bethlehem and Ramallah and travel to holy sites together.

As we walked to the *mikvah* through Muslim neighborhoods, our Arab friends greeted us with, "Good morning, Bible." They called the Rav "Bible" not because he was so pious but because his Hebrew name was Shraga Feivel, and they couldn't pronounce Feivel, so they called him "Bible" instead. It always made us laugh. One very nice Palestinian man, Rashad Jabarin, began sending his teenage sons over to help us with errands and babysitting. After a few months, we allowed them to take Yehuda, and later Michael, downstairs to the swings, while Suri and Leah were in school. This gave the Rav and me some quiet moments in which to work.

Yasir Jabarin was the older of the two boys. He was mischievous by nature—always up to something. Sufian, his younger brother, was just the opposite. Quiet and sensitive, we could always count on him. Sufian was also fun, and Yehuda and Michael spent time laughing with him as he translated Arab cartoons for them. The two brothers became part of our extended family.

On one occasion the Rav wanted to visit the Shiloah spring, which has served as a spiritual ritual bath since biblical times. But the Intifada, the Islamist-led uprising that had started in the occupied territories, was raging, making a trip to the spring dangerous. Once again, the Jabarin family showed their generous spirit by using their influence to help get us there safely.

Many years later, the Rav was sitting next to Yehuda on a plane, engrossed in a copy of Time magazine, when he suddenly stopped reading. "What is Rashad doing in this magazine?" he asked our son with some astonishment. Yehuda looked down at the photo the Rav was referring to, of a suicide bomber. As the Rav read on, it turned out that the photo wasn't of Rashad at all but of our sensitive and trustworthy babysitter, Sufian. Not only had this young man blown himself up, he had done so right in our old neighborhood. The force of the explosion was so great it set nearby traffic on fire and blew out the windows on buildings a block away. Twenty-four people died as a result of this violent act.

Disbelief doesn't begin to describe the Rav's reaction to the news. How could someone so kind do something so tragic? How does someone so caring and thoughtful become capable of taking the lives of others? The moment heightened the Rav's sense of urgency about bringing Kabbalah to the world, so that the consciousness of "Love thy Neighbor" could replace a mindset of vengeance and hate.

That tragedy still lay years in the future. At the time, among our family's most pleasurable outings were the regular visits we paid to the graves of righteous souls. We went once on the fifteenth day of each month and again on the day before the New Moon. This is one of the beautiful things about living in Israel. Within just a few hours to the north or south we could visit ancient sites inhabited by some of the greatest kabbalistic masters of all time.

We didn't have money, and we didn't have much else to do. In those days, there was little by way of entertainment in Jerusalem, even if our financial resources weren't so limited. There were no movie theaters, no shows, few restaurants, and no television or radio. This meant that we all looked forward to our trips when we talked to the sages. We drove in our tiny used Fiat, we nicknamed "Chitty Chitty Bang Bang," to visit the graves of the Ari, Rabbi Akiva, Rav Shimon, and the other holy and wise tzadikim buried in Safed or Mount Meron. We also went on their *yartzeit*—the anniversary of their deaths. The Zohar explains that this is a window in time when a soul connection becomes especially available.

Back then, these gravesites weren't big attractions—not like today, when busloads of men, women, and children arrive all day long, and you can barely get in. The cemeteries were empty and quiet. We would take Leah and Suri when they were not in school, our babies, a blanket, and a tablecloth to lay on the floor by Rabbi Akiva. We set out a basket and enjoyed a picnic lunch or dinner. When they were old enough, Yehuda and Michael would say "We're going to visit Rav Shimon." They were six or seven years old before they realized that these *tzadikim* had long since passed over from this physical world.

I have a lovely recollection of a time when the Rav and I took a *tzadikim* trip together, just the two of us. We went to visit the Ari, and it was pouring rain. The Rav rolled up his pants, and I took off my shoes and socks before we ran down the stairs to the courtyard where the Ari was buried. When we got there, we saw that there were two freshly lit candles waiting for us in a metal candle lantern. No one else was around, and because of the deluge it would have been difficult for us to light candles ourselves. It was a "Wow!" moment. In fact, almost every place we went that day in the rain, there were two freshly lit candles waiting for us. We saw it as a sign that we were being assisted from above.

Every time we travelled to the *tzadikim*, there were different lessons to be learned. Sometimes we were so involved in the spiritual aspect of our excursions we failed to deal with physical things like checking how much gas was in the car. This was primarily my responsibility, as I did most of the driving. Often when we visited Safed, we wouldn't realize the tank was nearly empty until we were already on our way back to Jerusalem. Each time it was the same question. "What are we going to do? Where are we going to find gas at two o'clock in the morning?" But the Light of the Creator always directed our journey, while still reminding us that, "Yes, you may be with the Light, but you still have to navigate this earthly terrain."

Once, near the Arab village of Jenin, we were driving on fumes. In desperation, we pulled into an Israeli army base. I drove over to the pumps and asked one of the soldiers, "Could you fill up our car with gas? We'll pay you."

The soldier looked at me as if I had four heads. "Listen," he said, "this is army gas. You're not allowed to use it, and I can't give it to you."

I pleaded with him. "Look," I said, pointing to the back seat. "I have children in the car. I don't have enough gas to get to Jerusalem, and there's no place along the way for us to fill up. So if you don't give us the gas, then please give us a place to stay. I'll pay you for that, too, because I can't get stuck without gas in the middle of the road in an Arab village."

He shook his head at our lack of foresight. "Okay, okay," he said, and pumped some gas into our car. Then he said, "I'm not doing this for you. I'm doing it for those kids." That's Israelis for you. They can be as hard as nails but if you need them in a pinch, they come through. The funny thing was (and we didn't know this at the time), gas from Israeli Army supplies was dyed red, so if it had ever leaked out of our car, everyone would have thought it was stolen.

The Rav didn't drive much, though one time when he was at the wheel, we paid a visit to the Dead Sea—not to the beach but to a place where we could park close to the water. He said to me, "I'm going to try to pull the car down where we can get a better view.

"Don't do that!" I shouted. "The wheels will get stuck in the mud."

But he was a Leo and didn't listen. So he drove that little Fiat about ten feet closer, just enough for the front wheels to sink into the sandy soil. He threw the transmission into reverse, but the back wheels just spun frantically, kicking up lots of debris. We went nowhere. "Oy! I made a little mistake," he said. "I thought this was a front wheel drive car!" It took us four hours with boards and rocks and both of us pulling and pushing to get the car out! We spent the entire time we could have been in the Dead Sea trying to find a way to free our vehicle.

That poor car really took a beating. It seemed like every year we had to change the engine or the transmission. When we finally decided to sell it, potential buyers thought it had been in an accident because the suspension was so shot. We certainly had loaded it with lots of heavy boxes of books. It was the only vehicle we had, and we worked it to death!

* * *

The Rav and I may have been finding our bearings in Israel, but we were still smoothing out the wrinkles in our relationship. The difficult arguments we'd had in New York about observance continued in Jerusalem. I had always been a free spirit. It's not that I didn't believe in the spiritual technology of Kabbalah. I did. But my approach to the rules tended to be relaxed, where the Rav's was strict. In addition to this, when the Rav sunk his teeth into an issue, he had a hard time letting go, which made it difficult to resolve an argument.

We enrolled the girls in a religious school where now they were required to learn Hebrew, not Yiddish. They worked through that issue, but then they were also forced to study English, despite the fact that it was their native language. This was ridiculous! English was the first class in the morning, and Leah, in particular, wanted to skip it and start later in the day but the school wouldn't bend the requirement for her. That's when the Rav stepped in. He fought for her and won. It helped Leah to know that the Rav was willing to stand up for her. Moments like this helped reinforce our bond. What's more, my girls now had two new baby brothers to play with.

We came to treasure many aspects of our early years in Jerusalem. Because the Rav worked in the evenings, he and I spent most of our days together. In the afternoon, when the girls got back from school, we would all go down to the playground. There, the Rav would work on his first book, Kabbalah for the Layman, while I played with the kids. Despite our disagreements, he and I didn't want to be away from each other for a moment, if we could help it.

Being largely alone in the world drew us together as a family.

* * *

I've made the point that the Rav was strict. And yes, he was stubborn, too. But perhaps it's more accurate to say that the Rav was primarily unyielding on behalf of the Light. This became much clearer to me during our first years together in Israel. In his earlier life he had lived according to religious conventions without fully understanding why.

Then from his teacher and his studies he learned that the rules of religious behavior are, in fact, given to us as opportunities to expand our consciousness so we can experience the Light in every aspect of life. Certainly he was still strict but now it was not just following rules for their own sake.

The Rav would say, "When this world was created, the Light of the Creator subjugated itself so that we could be co-creators of our destiny." The Light cannot enter our world, which like the moon has no Light of its own, unless we flip the switch to reveal it. We do this with our consciousness by using our free will to desire the Light more than all the other things that pull at our attention. Through our consciousness, through our efforts, and through kabbalistic tools, we draw Light for ourselves and at the same time for the whole world. These instruments include prayers, meditations, certain windows of time, and tools like the Zohar. They all work in different ways.

The Rav was hungry for the Light. "The way to remove chaos, the way to remove darkness is by turning on the Light," he would say. He was adamant that his observance wasn't about religion. Even though he looked religious to many, the consciousness motivating him was something different. According to Kabbalah, revealing Light lessens the darkness, hastens the coming of the Messiah, and brings us all closer to the removal of chaos in the world.

The Rav's desire was a driving force that made our lives and our choices unpredictable. The Rav never made a decision for himself or even for our family, but instead he sought to jump on every opportunity the Light sent his way. It's a good thing that standing still is not in my DNA, so I was comfortable with our nomadic life. But for my daughters it was another story. Both girls are earth signs who cherish stability.

* * *

The Rav would awaken every night at three o'clock in the morning, open the Zohar, and study. For as long as I can remember, he slept very little—maybe four or five hours a night. Even if he went to bed at midnight, he would still arise at three o'clock in the morning to learn. This wasn't because he had no time to study during the day, nor was it simply a reflection of his piety. He wanted to take advantage of those windows of time in a day when one can access the Light more freely. The Zohar says that whoever gets up at midnight to study from its pages plugs themselves into a conduit of mercy. The Rav never missed such an opportunity, which sometimes made scheduling impossible.

Holidays, too, provide significant opportunities to access Light. Yom Kippur offers a particularly opportune moment when the human soul is granted access to the level of Binah, a storehouse of spiritual energy. Ordinarily we can't approach the top three levels—Keter, Chochmah, or Binah—they're out of our reach. On Yom Kippur, however, we can draw the abundance of Binah into this physical world. The Rav would call this "Light we cannot imagine, accessible beyond our wildest dreams." "On Yom Kippur, there's no Satan consciousness," he would say. "We don't need challenges to elevate ourselves. The bank vault is open, and you can come in and take as much as you want."

One incident in 1973 at the start of the Yom Kippur War illustrates the Rav's uncompromising pursuit of the Light. The enemies of Israel chose to attack the nation on Yom Kippur, the holiest of holidays, when the population was fasting and deep in prayer. On that day, October 6, we were taking a break at home in the afternoon before returning to synagogue for the final Neilah prayers. Our young boys were downstairs with Rashad's sons. When we first heard the air raid sirens, the Rav said, "Someone just hit the wrong button." But then the sirens went off again, and now there were army Jeeps in the streets and soldiers with bullhorns shouting, "Close your blinds! Close your blinds! Close your blinds!"

We yelled out the window to Yasir and Sufian to bring the boys and come upstairs. We were under attack!

The Rav refused to go down to the bomb shelter, the *miklat* in the basement of the building. "Soon it will be the time for us to go back to synagogue," he said. "And everybody is in the bomb shelter! This is an amazing thing to see in this neighborhood," he continued sarcastically, referring to our observant neighbors. The Rav was incensed. "It's Yom Kippur, and everybody is listening to their radios and talking on their telephones? What is this?"

"A war is going on," I reminded him. "They're all huddled in the *miklat*. They're afraid."

"What's that got to do with anything?" he replied. "Let's get the Torah Scroll from the synagogue so we can finish the final prayers."

"Are you kidding?" I said, "No one is interested in prayers. They're not interested in anything except whether or not we'll be bombed."

"Go to the shelter and talk to somebody," he told me.

I found the local rabbi in the *miklat* with everyone else. I asked him, "Is there a possibility that someone can bring a Bible Scroll here so we can finish the final prayers? It's not that far to the synagogue—just a few blocks away."

He shook his head. "This is war. We don't have to pray. God will forgive us. It's more important that we stay here in the shelter and protect our lives than finish the final prayers." So I asked him for the keys to the synagogue. War or no war, I volunteered to walk over and pick up the Scroll myself. But that was impossible. In Orthodox circles, a woman is not permitted to carry the Scroll.

Eventually, about a half hour before Neilah was to begin, we found a little study space that had a Scroll and finished the prayers with a handful of brave people. For the Rav, the most upsetting part of this incident was how everyone had lost sight of their faith. He couldn't understand why they cared more about their safety than they did about drawing down the immense Light available to them on Yom Kippur.

Not to access this Light, especially during a period of darkness like wartime, meant missing a huge opportunity. Yom Kippur opens up a storehouse of infinite Light. What could offer more protection than that? Connecting to that Light could stop the war, not huddling in a shelter. Fear denies the benevolence of the Creator. A kabbalist cannot trust fear.

The Rav learned this from the story about Rav Brandwein ignoring snipers every night on the road to study with Rav Ashlag. The Rav also had his own direct experience of Rav Brandwein's fearlessness and certainty a month or two after the Six-Day War, when tensions were still running high between Arabs and Israelis. While the two men were studying together in Tel Aviv late one night, Rav Brandwein stood up suddenly and announced they were going to Bethlehem to visit Rachel's tomb. Right then, at two o'clock in the morning! He said it with such conviction that Feivel Gruberger couldn't argue with him—even though the city was in Palestinian hands and entry to the tomb was barred due to renovations.

"That makes no difference," Rav Brandwein replied, waving away his student's objections. Stubbornness on behalf of the Light is obviously a defining quality for kabbalists! They drove through the darkness to Bethlehem on deserted roads. When they arrived a few hours later, the gates to Rachel's tomb were locked but Rav Brandwein was unperturbed. He sat on a small bench and waited calmly. At dawn, a guard appeared and asked if he could open the gates for them. Inside the tomb, Rav Brandwein stood in meditative reverence for quite some time, sending Light of protection to areas in need.

Now it was the Rav who was revealing the power of Kabbalah's tools. When the Rav had a conviction, not even war could change his mind. His stubbornness was evolving. It was becoming certainty. And as each opportunity presented itself, he climbed another rung on the ladder.

* * *

Chasing the Light was not always about putting yourself into dangerous situations. Sometimes it involved behavior that looked silly to those who did not know the Rav. One night in Jerusalem during the holiday of Sukkot, we read about a goat that came to the Ari and said that it had finished its tikkun and wanted to get *shechted* (slaughtered according to kosher practice) so that it could elevate itself. In this way it could return to the higher state it had occupied before it reincarnated as a goat. Within the confines of that time period, its soul could be released from its animal body. According to the Ari, there are specific windows of time when non-human aspects of nature—plant life, animals, and inanimate objects—can elevate their souls to the next level, giving new meaning to the saying, "For everything there is a season."

We had read that passage from the Ari together, and the next morning when we returned from the Kotel, we had a surprise. There was a donkey in our Sukkah, the temporary shelter we had built. The Rav yelled, "Donkey in the Sukkah! Donkey in the Sukkah! Hurry up! We have to make Kiddush for this donkey." So the Rav, Suri, and I started running around like crazy people, looking for the wine, the cup, and the cake we needed for the blessing. We made Kiddush for the donkey, and Suri and I had a good laugh before it wandered off. The Rav, for all his playful sense of humor, also saw this ritual as an opportunity he was not going to miss.

* * *

In 1973, while we were living in that same four story walk-up on Jabotinsky, an elderly woman climbed the long flights of stairs to our apartment, knocked on our door, and asked me for food. Although we didn't have much, I said, "Sure," and made her some sandwiches.

She thanked me and left.

A few minutes later, the Rav walked in, and I told him what had happened. "Why didn't you give her money?" he asked me.

"Because she didn't ask for money!" This seemed logical to me.

"Don't you imagine that when someone comes in and asks you for food, obviously they need money?"

"You may be right. I hadn't thought of it that way."

He shoved some bills into his pocket and ran down to the street after this woman but she had disappeared. He spent a good half hour looking for her, to no avail. The Rav was certain that she was an apparition of Elijah the Prophet. Why else would an old woman walk up four flights of stairs to knock on our door and ask for food? He came back upset that he couldn't find her. He could only imagine how much Light of the Creator could be revealed by the appearance of Elijah.

Just like the Israelites following the Cloud of Glory in the desert, routine was never an option for us. In fact, the Rav used to say, "Some people live one day in seventy years but other people live seventy years in one day." We were in the latter group. Our lives were definitely not predictable or mundane! But this pressure was helping shape the Rav into who he was meant to be.

* * *

There was a Yeshiva up on Mount Zion where a group of hippies hung out. Mostly in their teens and early twenties, many had come over from the United States hoping to find themselves. They congregated around the school, and when the Rav went up the mountain to teach at the nightclub in the evenings, he started talking to them and taking them under his wing.

A handful of these young men began coming by to study with the Rav at three o'clock in the morning—the right time to access the Light of mercy. He loved this. He loved it when someone wanted to learn. Even though we were living on pennies ourselves, we took in some of these young men, fed them, housed them, and sent them back to the Yeshiva the next day. Suri reminded me that her earliest memories of Israel always included brothers in addition to her own.

The Rav's enthusiastic embrace of these youths gave me an idea.

Up until this time, most of the people Rav Brandwein had taught were family—his son-in-law, his son, and then his niece's husband, the Rav—all learned men. Three people was a nice number for a group learning Kabbalah in secret. But since that late fall of 1971, that first year we spent in Israel, a notion had been germinating in my mind that I needed to share with the Rav.

He had been teaching me Kabbalah since our momentous breakfast at Ratner's. Not in a formal setting, or from the texts (since I couldn't read or understand Hebrew), or in the wee hours of the morning the way he had learned from Rav Brandwein. Instead, as life presented us with an opportunity he explained specific kabbalistic concepts. Over many long days and evenings he shared this knowledge.

But something about this didn't sit right with me. Compelled to bring up what I knew would be a difficult subject, I asked him to take a walk with me in the park. This, of course, piqued his curiosity.

"Okay," he said once we got there. "Spit it out. What's troubling you? Have I done something wrong?"

"No, not at all," I replied. And then I launched into it.

"I know you've been asking yourself, where do we go from here? I also know that Rav Brandwein and Rav Ashlag followed the same traditional course of teaching Kabbalah as kabbalists have adhered to for two thousand years. Only married men over the age of forty who are already trained in Talmud are permitted to be part of this group.

"But your teacher and his teacher before him," I continued, "have succeeded in removing many of the veils that made Kabbalah too difficult for the uninitiated to absorb. Because of their work, now even a person like me can understand it." I began trembling. "So I believe you have to take their efforts to the next level." There. I'd said it.

"What are you trying to tell me?" he asked me, his brow furrowing with concern.

"What I'm saying," I replied, "is that there are a lot of people out there who would be interested in this knowledge if they knew it existed. If you can teach me, then anybody should be able to learn it, right? I think the time has come for you to open Kabbalah to every man, woman, and child who has a desire to learn it. Why should I be the only one? Think of how much Light this could bring to the world, how much good you could do."

My husband went pale. He staggered over to a nearby bench and sat down, holding his head as if it were spinning. After collecting his thoughts, he looked at me and in a loud voice, oblivious to people passing by, he said, "Do you know what you are saying? Tell me it's a joke. Tell me you're not serious. Where did you get this idea from? Forget it! It's impossible! It just won't work."

* * *

The Rav had taught me the concept of Binding by Striking regarding the very first verse of the Bible, Genesis A 1:1. The explanation given by the Zohar is as follows:

> *With the beginning of the manifestation of the King's will, that is, when the King desired to emanate and create the world, a hard spark made an engraving upon the Supernal Light. This hard spark, which emanated from the most concealed of all concealed things, from the secret of the Endless Light, took a shapeless form.*

We discover from the Zohar that by striking something we actually connect with it and draw it toward ourselves. Rav Ashlag explained the concept of Binding by Striking by comparing it to someone hitting a rock with another rock, thereby creating a spark. Why does a spark result?

The Zohar says everything that ultimately becomes revealed does so because there is a Force—the Light—that wants to be expressed. One way it is revealed is through resistance. When we hit a rock with another, a spark emerges because the rock resists the impact. Whenever two entities meet and one resists the other a spark emerges, although sometimes we see it and sometimes we don't. This spark reveals Light that's already there—it creates a circuit of energy between two people who may be in conflict with one another.

Does this mean we should oppose another person just to create a circuit of energy? No. But when we listen sincerely, as the Rav did on that fateful day, and engage in questions to better understand the other person, our questioning provides the kind of resistance that produces a spark and reveals Light. People don't remember someone who only wants to tell them things but has no time for questions or feedback. Such a person will not make an impact because there has to be an exchange of positions to create resistance. If the energy flows only in one direction, there is no contact but when each person becomes both sharer and the receiver, the circuit of energy emerges. Contact happens through resistance, which ultimately creates a greater exchange of ideas. Rav Ashlag described this phenomenon in an essay entitled Article on Freedom.

> *The more opposition, contradiction, and criticism there is, the more wisdom and understanding can proliferate, and things become clear and easier to understand [...] The basis for ideas and intellectual success is disunity and disagreement. [...] And if argument and criticism disappear, all ideas and intellectual advancement will cease, and the source of wisdom will, as we understand, dry up from the world.*

Thought is so powerful that it can move people. God's sharing takes the form of the Light of *Ein Sof* (the Endless Light), which encompasses every force that exists in this world. It includes anything that wants to move outwardly from one place into another. Whether our hand strikes a rock or we want to influence someone, this is the same Force of *Ein Sof.* When someone has an idea, and he wants everyone to believe in it, he expands and trics to influence others. When a number of people accept this thought, there has been a manifestation, an extension of the thought into others.

It took a few minutes for the Rav to regain his composure after his outburst. He seemed incapable of responding to my suggestion. Finally he closed his eyes and began to meditate, connecting to his master and his master's master. Their answer was unusually clear. "Listen to Karen for she is an incarnation of …." (He wasn't allowed to tell me who this was.)

No matter. Despite what his teachers were telling him, he resisted. We dare not take this step. It was beyond imagination. "You realize this has never been done before," he said.

"Of course I do," I replied softly, "but I think it has never been done before because you and I have never been there to do it! This is something we need to try. Why not?" This has always been my nature. To push up against established notions and see if they move. It can't hurt to try.

"You know," he responded, "that we're going to be ridiculed and humiliated. We're going to be outcasts. People will want to hurt you. They won't want this knowledge." He argued that the wrath that had rained down upon us in New York would be nothing compared to the towering rage from every corner of the Jewish world if he opened

Kabbalah to everyone who wanted to learn it. "I'm not sure we can withstand the storm," he admitted.

Given the Rav's upbringing, he found it difficult to venture outside the norm. He responded negatively to the very idea until he could find a way past the programming that had shaped his every decision and action. This wasn't easy to do. But I hadn't come from a coherent, self-contained world like my husband, so I wasn't tied to the strictures he felt compelled to follow. I hadn't been raised since birth with sacred rules that forbade behavior like intermarriage or teaching Kabbalah to the uninitiated.

Though I was naïve and didn't understand the full import of my suggestion, my life had done a good job of preparing me for adventure. My childhood was full of turmoil and instability. I loved the road less traveled. It was easy for me to make a radical suggestion—much easier than it was for the Rav to accept it. So I waited for my husband to come around.

As he wrestled with my idea, he cautioned me that the path I suggested would be a lonely one. Although we could find comfort in the *tzadikim*, there would be few living people to whom we could turn for help. Our only consistent source of support would be each other.

"Okay," I persisted. "But at least we will have done something in this world."

The dilemma I had presented was difficult for him to reconcile. Aside from the hateful reaction he so correctly predicted, I had asked him to challenge a venerated, 2,000-year-old paradigm. He must have been asking himself, "Am I really going to be the one who dares to break open Kabbalah? *Am I really going to be the one who takes it outside the Orthodox world that kept it secret for millennia?*" I could only imagine the struggle taking place within the Rav given the awe he felt for Rav Ashlag and Rav Brandwein and for this wisdom that sages had taught privately for so long.

But make the decision he did. "Okay," he said, eventually. "I'm willing to try. Let's see what happens."

How did he choose to leap across the void to the next ladder? Perhaps he followed the recommendation of his teachers that he listen to me. Or perhaps it was his own fierce longing for the Light. Or perhaps he harkened back to an earlier time when he had balked at packing boxes of books and Rav Brandwein had told him, "We will reveal more Light doing so than we will in study. For if you and I study one hour, that's one hour of study, but if we pack these books and 100 people study one hour from them, that is 100 hours of study that reveals Light in the world."

This extraordinary moment in our lives would eventually affect millions of people and shift our universal consciousness. At first, the Rav resisted my idea. There certainly was a spark as he pushed back. But once he understood that the Light of Kabbalah wanted to be revealed, he knew what it would take and he was just stubborn enough to do it.

Once he had clarity and certainty, he began expanding its reach as he interested others in learning Kabbalah. And that's how the Rav started teaching this wisdom—in the early morning hours to a few of the young men who had been hanging around the Yeshiva. Eventually, several years later, this impulse expanded exponentially to the uninitiated masses in Israel. The seed of the Kabbalah Centre was planted.

* * *

Even viewed in hindsight, this was not a continuous path forward. We struggled mightily during those early few years in Israel. Finally, shortly after the Yom Kippur War, when Michael was only a few months old, we decided we'd had enough. We gave up our apartment in Jerusalem, left those first few students behind, and rented a house in Fort Lee, New Jersey.

We moved for many reasons. First of all, with a four-month-old and a toddler, we wanted to be away from the possibility of more wars. Besides, we were barely scraping by financially, and we thought life might be easier in the United States. Fort Lee was a secular community, so our marriage would not be an issue.

The Rav set up shop as a life coach and spiritual counselor, helping people to apply kabbalistic wisdom to their personal struggles and careers. Although we didn't know it at the time, this was an early model for the way our teachers would come to work with students. The Rav didn't just want to teach Kabbalah, he wanted to make the world better by teaching people the wisdom and tools of Kabbalah so they could improve their lives.

How did prospective students learn about the Rav? Some responded to an advertisement he had placed in the local newspaper, while others connected to him through word of mouth. I remember one man, an alcoholic, had joined AA but was struggling with the spiritual aspects of the program. He came to the Rav for help so he could continue to go to meetings.

* * *

Of all of us, Leah was the happiest to be back in the United States. She was in the 6th grade then, about twelve years old, and she hadn't adjusted well to Orthodox life or to the domestic turbulence as the Rav and I struggled to find common ground. On our return, Leah decided to go live with her father. Despite the fact that none of us wanted Leah to move out, it was clear that she had made up her mind. Of course, I was very upset about this, but I knew that our life wasn't right for her. Of all people, I appreciated her need for stability. She did visit us from time to time. I missed her very much, and I was thrilled years later when eventually she came back into the fold and married one of our teachers.

For the rest of us, however, the return to the United States turned out to be a disappointment. We no longer had Leah living with us, which felt like a major loss. And after two years, we realized that we didn't love living in the United States either. It wasn't providing us with the environment we needed to flourish, nor did it seem to be the right place for the early seeds of Kabbalah to take hold. And so we returned to Jerusalem, a city the Rav truly loved.

And we began once again.

CHAPTER 7:

THE RAV COMES INTO HIS OWN

For those who want to know who the Rav *really* was, I'd have to say that he was three different people. First was the father. I have such sweet memories of him in the early evenings before setting off to work. That's when the Rav used to lie in bed with Yehuda and Michael and tell them what we called "Shragi stories." To help them fall asleep he would make up the adventures of a little boy named Shragi (his alter-ego?) who rode around on a big white horse. As a child, the Rav had been a big fan of John Wayne and Westerns like *The Lone Ranger* so this gave him and the boys great pleasure.

Then there was the husband. My husband. Sometimes I felt I was the only person in the world to whom he really listened. With me he was affectionate and loveable and vulnerable—and very funny. He completely lowered his guard around me, and I did the same for him.

Finally, there was the teacher. When I first challenged my husband to teach Kabbalah to everyone and he eventually agreed, I don't believe he fully realized what this would entail. But as the idea grew in him, I'm sure his own teacher came to mind. As the Rav later wrote, "The master told me that I would have to be the one to disseminate the once-forbidden Zohar and the secrets of immortality to the world for the first time in human history." Once he stepped into this role, once he welcomed the idea of teaching Kabbalah to everyone, he evolved into the person he was meant to be—fearless, determined, and unstoppable.

Thanks to his certainty and courage, my husband was able to accomplish what no one else could. "This is what I believe in, this is where I'm going," he would say, "and this is what's going to happen." This was a blueprint for how we conducted our lives. He would decide on a direction. Sometimes I would suggest a different course but he would say, "No, that's not the way. It's not my ego; I know I'm right!" he would claim, and most of the time he was. When he decided on something, there was no changing his mind. Certainly the Rav could never be swayed by compliments, or impressed by money, or intimidated by power. That just wasn't in his nature.

After a while, I learned to see that the Rav's vision was extraordinarily clear in most situations, although not necessarily when it came to everyday decisions, which often fell to me. But when it came to seeing to the heart of things, it was as if he were looking through water. I think this was due to his immersion in the wisdom. It blessed him with insight—*re'eh*. It shaped him into a visionary. It made the Rav the Rav.

* * *

My husband warned me from the beginning that we would face daunting—and perhaps overwhelming—challenges. Once he embraced the idea of teaching Kabbalah to the uninitiated, he never imagined even for a minute, that ours would be an easy life. But he didn't hesitate. When we came back to Israel in 1975, the Rav returned to teaching interested young people, starting with the hippies who continued to congregate around the Yeshiva. The Rav felt a responsibility to these young people, stating on more than one occasion that society had failed them in their efforts to find the Light, and this is why some of them had turned to drugs.

His was an unorthodox perspective on drug abuse. Perhaps the best example was an incident with a young man who showed up very stoned at one of our gatherings and started screaming and lunging at the Rav. One of our teachers tried to hold him back but the Rav said, "No, no. Let him come at me. He's right. He's upset with us because we've let him down." He didn't deflect the anger but took full responsibility for it. "You're right," he told the man. "I accept what you're saying. Let's talk about it."

The Rav believed that the rational mind is a prison from which our higher consciousness knows it must escape. Transcendence is a spiritual impulse. Drugs are a response to this desire, and they're often taken by sensitive souls who understand that this world of darkness is not all there is. They simply seek the Light. The problem is not their motivation but the fact that drugs aren't the right tool for the job and are ultimately dangerous to the body.

From the Kabbalistic point of view, whatever is temporary is considered an illusion. A drug "high" quickly wears off, leaving the user in a lower state of consciousness than before. Addicts become slaves to this illusion, but the Rav believed they should not be condemned for this. By way of an alternative, society needed sane, socially condoned methods of transcendence that didn't harm the body, like Kabbalah. By connecting these young people to kabbalistic wisdom, the Rav sought to wean them from their destructive drug habits, replacing them with an addiction to the Light. This, he firmly believed, was the best way to help a person on drugs.

Another of the Rav's main concerns in the mid-1970s was that so many young Jews were turning to Eastern mystical traditions because they couldn't find what they were looking for within the confines Orthodox Judaism. Some young Israelis were traveling to India and the United States in search of a more satisfying New Age spiritual practice after they'd finished their stint in the army. In Israel itself, society was divided between those who were Orthodox or ultra-Orthodox and those who were completely secular—disconnected from Judaism. There was little middle ground for people who wanted to explore spirituality without having to belong to an Orthodox sect.

One of the Rav's intentions when he first started teaching was to bring these disaffected young people back home. He did this not by asking them to study learned texts like the Study of the Ten Luminous Emanations but by teaching basic elements of spirituality. He believed that once people got a taste of what Kabbalah had to offer, they would want to return to Judaism. One of the Rav's founding principles was that one should never reject people for pursuing an alternative faith. He practiced religious tolerance, having absorbed the lesson from Rav Brandwein that love and human dignity are at the root of Kabbalah.

The stage was set for a leader to emerge, and my husband, the Rav, rose to the occasion to fulfill his destiny. He started teaching three young men, then five. They would come to our apartment to learn. In those days, the Rav's command of Modern Hebrew was still limited, so he taught the classes in English. Eventually, he did teach from texts by Rav Ashlag and Rav Isaac Luria written in Aramaic and Hebrew, books we published ourselves. As a teacher, he created an atmosphere that was charged with excitement and promise. It was magical.

* * *

One young man who came to study Kabbalah was completely smitten by it. We let him stay with us in our apartment and absorbed him into our family—he became one of the "brothers" Suri referred to in the previous chapter. After six months the Rav said, "Okay, now you go out and teach." Then the next serious student came, and then one after that. We started to expand.

With more students coming for classes, our small apartment became quite crowded for our growing family, and it was hard on our kids. One room was packed with

5,000 copies of books, some of which we were hoping to ship to the United States. The Rav and I claimed one bedroom, and Suri, Yehuda, and Michael shared the other one. The young students we took in would bed down on a couch in the living room.

These were tiny rooms, the furniture sparse, and often not fully functional. Our bed had a broken leg that we kept fixing with nails and a hammer, but it kept on collapsing. There was only one closet in the apartment, and our bedroom was missing a door. The stove needed pliers to turn the gas on and off. There was no money for these creature comforts, so we ignored the inconvenience.

Finally, in 1975 I asked the Rav, "Why don't we find a place where you can teach?" The site of the Rav's first outside lecture was Beit Tsiyonei America (American Zionist House) affiliated with the Zionist Organization of America. He also taught a class at a B'nai B'rith facility. Both were in Tel Aviv.

We got in touch with Rabbi Kahana, the man we'd met at the airport who had been so kind to us. Once again he found a way to help. He managed to get us a stipend to advertise our classes. He loved what the Rav was doing, so he reached out to someone who had rooms for rent on Bograshov Street in the heart of Tel Aviv, not far from the Shuk Carmel—the large, bustling outdoor market.

This was the first place where Kabbalah was taught full-time. It was a small space—just 1,500 square feet—on the first floor. We used the vestibule for registration, and behind that a glass partition created a classroom for

40 students, and another, smaller room accommodated 25 more. The office had a tiny kitchen with a hotplate. We couldn't conduct services there—it was too small—but this was the beginning of the Kabbalah Centre as we know it today.

* * *

So there was the Rav, in Israel of all places, teaching Kabbalah, which had never been taught before to groups of uninitiated men and women together in the same room. And in English. Besides that, he insisted that to follow the religious laws of Judaism just because they were written that way was crazy; students needed to be taught their kabbalistic significance. He reiterated the principle that there is no coercion in spirituality; God doesn't compel anyone to be religious. It was a matter of choice. God is all giving and loving—not punitive. These revolutionary ideas attracted secular young Israelis who had rejected the strictures of Orthodoxy and felt alienated from their own religion. Kabbalah was just what they had been looking for.

As expected, the religious backlash began almost immediately. How dare the Rav do something so sacrilegious as to teach Kabbalah to people who were uninformed? And mixing genders in the same room? It was a *shonda*—a cause for shame. The establishment wouldn't tolerate it, secular people didn't know what to think about it, and we were caught in the middle.

"The Rav is a charlatan!" they declared. The problem with this line of attack, however, was that he had been raised by an Orthodox family, had attended Yeshiva, had been ordained a rabbi, and had studied for years with a revered kabbalist. His credentials were difficult to discredit. If they couldn't claim that he didn't know what he was talking about, they could say that he had gone mad.

It was at times like these that the Rav reminded himself that throughout history, teachers of Kabbalah had suffered abuse. He would be no exception. But as he and his teacher used to say, "If one has not undergone the pain of spreading the knowledge of Kabbalah, one has done nothing. Only Kabbalah can bring peace. When we speak of Kabbalah, we will naturally bring forth those who oppose us. In fact, it is a sign that we are doing our work correctly." So he kept on, unfazed by the attacks.

Religious groups live in their own closed communities where they support each other for all practicing the same way. But we were outsiders, so they looked for ways to undermine us. Once the hostility began in earnest, the Rav teased me, "I told you so." And I teased him back: "So you told me so. So what? What can happen?" This was my rebellious streak talking. And I was strong—as long as he was by my side. As long as we had each other, we were going to be okay. And while the criticism grew more intense, the number of students also kept growing.

We formulated an entry-level course so that students could readily absorb the wisdom. We broke it down into pieces they could digest and then apply to their own lives.

We talked about the creation of the world in ways people had never heard before. We discussed restriction of the Desire to Receive, proactive behavior, and sharing. We explained how the tools of Kabbalah can elevate consciousness. We introduced concepts like reincarnation, astrology, and meditation, and we offered spiritual tools like immersion in the *mikvah* for spiritual cleansing.

Traditionally, only religious men used immersion in this way, yet we taught it to everyone. Rabbis objected to our bringing women into the *mikvah* but from his teacher the Rav learned that the *mikvah* can help everyone remove the energy of negativity, regardless of gender. There are those who believe that women didn't need to be *that* spiritual, the Rav was not among them.

Members of the conservative community said all kinds of things about the Rav and me to discredit us. Someone sent a photo of us to the police, claiming we had gotten married while the Rav was still married to Rivka. While the rest of the world was singing along to "Staying Alive" by the Bee Gees—it was the 70s, after all—we were actually struggling to stay alive. But despite the poverty, the hardship, and the slings and arrows from his own community, the Rav did not lose his certainty. He continued to see every person as a vessel, and his task was to ignite the spark of Light waiting to be revealed. So we kept on. One person at a time. Growing and keeping on. Keeping on, no matter what.

Our enemies went to Rabbi Kahana and complained, "How can you help these people? Don't you see what they're doing?" Some wrote articles about how destructive the teachings were, and others sent out word that the Rav should be barred from teaching anywhere. Friends were few and far between, though each one made a big difference. Esau Habash, a Christian Arab with a printing plant in Jerusalem, helped us solve the problem of the 5,000 books crammed into our Jerusalem apartment. Esau said, "I have a warehouse," and he opened it for us.

It was difficult for us to commute between Jerusalem and Tel Aviv now that the Rav was teaching classes two or three nights a week. Today's modern highway between the two cities didn't exist; we traveled the back roads, and it took a long time. The boys were little, and some nights I left them with Suri or Yasir and Sufian, Rashad's sons. Finally, we decided it was just too much of a schlep, so we moved to Tel Aviv.

Sometimes I think the Rav took on my karma when we got married because our life together began to feel like my itinerant childhood. We moved first to Ramat Gan, an area just east of Tel Aviv. Then we moved again to Givatayim, another community east of Tel Aviv in a metropolitan area known as Gush Dan. Then we moved yet again to the ultra-Orthodox neighborhood of Bnei Brak. Change was the only constant in our lives, so much so that—to the degree that eventually, years later, Suri decided that she wanted to live on a Kibbutz so she could stay in one high school. Shades of my own past.

And still people came and came and came, and our teaching community grew and grew and grew.

As interest in Kabbalah blossomed, some of our students became teachers and began to do outreach, traveling to other Israeli cities. Sometimes they took the bus north to Haifa, an hour and a half away. Sometimes they would teach in Be'er Sheva, two hours south by bus in the Negev Desert. Sometimes, they went to Jerusalem. Soon we opened a satellite educational center in Haifa.

* * *

Eitan Yardeni was 17 when he first came into contact with the Rav. He was curious about spirituality and was asking deep questions at this early age. His older brother, Eliyahu, had already become a teacher at the Centre. Even before Eitan started taking classes, he had a meaningful encounter with the Rav.

Eliyahu had invited us to their parents' home for dinner. Eitan sat there quietly, watching us from the corner of his eye. Later, he told us that he'd felt awe at that moment but he didn't let on. He just looked. And connected. After dinner, as we were leaving, he shook the Rav's hand and that was it for him—much the same way it had been for Shraga Feivel Gruberger when he touched Rav Brandwein two decades earlier. Eliyahu told me that right after that encounter, the Rav said to him, "You know, your brother Eitan just told me that he wants to be a Chevre," even though Eitan hadn't uttered a word.

Eliyahu was our first Chevre. This term evolved from the Hebrew word chaverim, meaning "group of friends."

The Zohar was revealed in this world through the power and unity of the chaverim—the ten people who studied with Rav Shimon. We adopted the term for teachers and staff who wanted to wholly dedicate themselves to the mission of teaching Kabbalah. Thus began the culture of the Kabbalah Centre clergy. The Chevre drew no salary, living like members of a Kibbutz: all the basics were provided for, so they were free to teach and be of service to people.

A few months later, Eliyahu's brother Eitan started taking classes at the Centre on Bograshov Street in Tel Aviv. After the first class he felt an "instant elevation." He couldn't sleep that night. And soon, he too was drawn to the work. Like many others who eventually became Chevre, Eitan also started coming to the Rav's Study of the Ten Luminous Emanations classes twice a week at four o'clock in the morning.

"We were in the middle of deep stuff," he told me, "which I didn't fully understand but the Light that I felt there, and the conviction that I felt from the Rav, they all made me feel that this was my home, my place. There was no question what I would do after the army. It was like clarity. I came to the Rav, and I said, 'I want to be here full time.'" Soon the Rav and I offered Eitan the opportunity to be in charge of administering the classes in Haifa.

And we kept on growing. By 1978, four hundred committed students were learning Kabbalah in Israel. We had what we considered huge classes—maybe 15, 20, or 25 people. The Rav and I continued our own spiritual adventures, visiting the graves of the *tzadikim* on their death anniversaries, however, now we brought groups of people, maybe fifty students at a time. We even visited Rav Ashlag and Rav Brandwein's graves. These trips were fulfilling and inspiring. Students could experience first-hand the energy of the *tzadikim* whom we'd talked about in class. It's also true that in a group of like-minded people, energy becomes amplified.

Two or three times a year we would celebrate Shabbat or conduct High Holiday retreats with a hundred students in Beit Meir, a religious settlement in the Jerusalem Hills, not far from that city, or in the village of Nir Etzion, a small settlement in the north, near Carmel. We all stayed together in facilities with a dining hall. We would eat, sleep, pray, learn, and sing together—a community in search of Light. Back then, this was a huge gathering for us, and we struggled to manage the logistics. I can only look back and laugh, since today thousands of people from all over the world regularly attend these kinds of events. In the early days, it was a challenge—but it was one we cherished.

As we took on more teachers, there were times when the Rav sensed their egos were becoming too involved—they became too personally attached or too excited. He confronted them to wake them up—he'd "give them on the head," as we said. He could be stern that way. "Do you remember who you are?" he would ask them. "Do you remember what the Light is? You cannot help people when the teaching becomes about you," he would remind them.

When he acted this way, sometimes I would object. But he would reply, "Karen, you don't know how critical this is for this person." So he gave it to them straight. And people either woke up and smelled the roses or they left because they couldn't tolerate what he was saying. With the Rav, what you saw was what you got; he was incapable of hiding his feelings, and he never pulled his punches.

* * *

Our young teachers all began their relationship with the Rav in much the same way. In the late 70's most were men in their early twenties. In one way or another, they had heard about Kabbalah from a friend, relative, or from an article attacking the Rav. Many of these young people were rebels—very common at that time in Israel—so the fact that the Rav ruffled the feathers of the establishment piqued their interest.

They came to classes once a week, alone or with friends. Many were still in the army, but they would find a way to leave their posts to listen to the Rav's lectures. "His talks were so inspiring, so mind boggling," one of the teachers commented. "I would have done anything to come to those lectures." Some had plans to travel or to find careers, and others had no plans at all—they were still figuring out what to do with their lives. But once they began participating in our programs and classes, it became clear to them that Kabbalah was what they wanted most of all. As they immersed themselves in this work, everything else disappeared.

Every chance they got, they came to study and help. When they were released from the army they usually got jobs to support themselves, and came to the Centre whenever they had free time. They developed a routine. They made their way to Tel Aviv to participate in a Study of the Ten Luminous Emanations class with the Rav at our apartment in the early morning. I would prepare some breakfast—cheese, eggs, an omelet, whatever I had on hand—and then they would go to work. At four o'clock, at the end of the work day, they would return to the Kabbalah Centre in Tel Aviv to set up the room for the evening classes, register students, and hang around afterward to speak to them. Then they would stay until midnight studying, before going home to sleep. Sometimes they slept at the Centre.

They didn't need more than a few hours' sleep. They were young, and jazzed by what they were learning.

Funded by growing book sales and donations, we soon had our first paid employees. These young men moved into an apartment only a short distance away, so they could study with the Rav in the morning. After they finished breakfast, they worked trying to place books in various bookstores and then returned in the evening to do whatever was needed at the Centre. They would travel with the Rav and me to the graves of the *tzadikim*. During the hours we spent in the car, we talked nonstop about Kabbalah and spirituality. That's just who we were.

Spending time together accelerated the learning for all of us. The students told me, "I learn Kabbalah simply by being with you and the Rav. I learn from watching you deal with situations." The Rav always had a lesson to learn or to teach. Every story had a message.

When our teachers asked if they could immerse themselves in the work of Kabbalah the way the Rav and I were doing, the Rav was circumspect. Working for the Centre is one thing, but making Kabbalah your life is another story. "Think about it," he told them. "Take a week. Take a month. This is a very serious move, so think it over."

Our teachers chafed at the restraint; this was the path they wanted for their lives. But the Rav was firm. "You should think it over," he repeated. Although they felt rejected, this only increased their desire. When they returned, the Rav was still hesitant. "You know," he told them, "You'll be burning all your bridges. There's no way back. I think you should give it another week."

After the third attempt, it was done. Students became teachers. Teachers became Chevre. Whatever we were doing, they were doing. We became a family through our shared purpose.

Why did the Rav gain so many devoted followers over the strenuous objections of the religious establishment? What was the attraction? First there was the wisdom, which had its own power. As one of our Chevre put it, "Just studying Kabbalah is unbelievable. It is so fulfilling, so energizing, so inspiring. We come out of Shabbat so charged with energy."

Then there was the Rav. Although he was demanding, our students and teachers could feel the love beneath his gruff exterior. He had a great capacity to give. He guided the students, nudging them into seeing what they needed to change in their lives. He pushed them to examine what was blocking the Light from being revealed in their life. Most of the time, he did this gently, depending on whom he was dealing with, although he could also be quite forceful.

A lot of what we teach in Kabbalah is about overcoming obstacles that block the Light. The Rav helped students believe they could surmount any barriers, whether it was their fears, their egos, or their internal darkness. He didn't just point out shortcomings; he framed them as opportunities for growth, and his positivity was contagious. One of our students who was suffering with family disruption, legal issues, and a divorce was walking down the hall dejected and miserable one day when the Rav looked at her and said, "You must know that in the end, everything will be good." And, of course, in the end, it was. She and her husband divorced amicably and remained friends. Her business took off, and the lawsuit she was wrestling with evaporated. Years later she became a Chevre.

The Rav used to say, "Our consciousness creates our reality." To that end he always kept an eye out for someone who was struggling and needed encouragement. Just a few words could open that person's consciousness to the possibilities that lay just beyond those challenges.

Above all, the Rav was certain. As his wife, this could be difficult, but it had a tremendous upside. When everyone and his brother was opposed to what we were doing, his inner strength carried us all through the storm. He himself was a force of nature. Yes, it's true that I loved him, but if I could be objective, I'd say that he was a beautiful human being.

People sensed it. When he walked into a room, you felt something ineffable shift. This happened wherever he went. How can I explain it? Each of us possesses spiritual energy, and all that work he had done and everything he had gone through amplified it for the Rav. In him it was a palpable force. It's not that he performed miracles but he imparted strength so that others could create their own. Despite his enlightened being, he came across as no better than anyone else; no more, no less; just the same. As my husband explained to one of the Chevre some years ago, "There is no difference between me and you. I've just had 30 more years of studying Kabbalah than you have." Elsewhere, he wrote, "I am not a prophet. The reason I have access to the information is because I pursue it."

The Rav understood that a leader should serve as an example. A good commander in the army, for example, eats after his soldiers have been fed. He has to be sensitive to those he is leading. The Rav told me that too often people don't see the person in front of them. "They see goals," he would say. "They see what they want to achieve but they don't see the importance of the people who assist them in achieving those goals."

A true leader, the Rav didn't care about being respected or what others thought of him—he had abandoned that need long before. He did what he believed was right without letting his certainty grow into the thought that he was better than anyone else. He created a revolution in the world, standing for the truth he had found with his teacher. He knew that many people would disagree with that truth but he also knew that the world would change eventually, and he was willing to pay a great personal price to be part of that change.

There was also his vision—his ability to see and predict. More than forty years ago, he would say to people and in public, "There will come a day when we will grow back our own organs, when we'll be able to transplant hearts and livers like we change car batteries and tires, when we'll be able to replace our old teeth with new ones. And eventually, we will reach the time of immortality and live forever."

In those days who talked of such things? I would warn him, "Don't say that!" But he was right. This ability to see the future came from what Kabbalah calls Divine Inspiration, which allows us to channel the Light of the Creator. We all have moments when we channel Light; Archimedes, Leonardo da Vinci, Mozart, and Einstein all gained regular access to something greater than themselves. This can happen simply because it is our destiny. Sometimes we channel Light because we care deeply for someone or something outside of ourselves.

For my husband it was all of the above, aided by his awareness of how the spiritual system works that he learned from his teacher. This often allowed him to know what would happen next. The Zohar says that when we devote genuine time to its study we can all see the bigger picture. All we have to do is analyze, explore, and examine with an open heart. Consider a seed. If you plant it in your yard, a plant will grow there. It's as simple as that, and it doesn't make the gardener a prophet.

Importantly, although the Rav's early training at Yeshiva was intellectual, once he met his teacher and started to learn Kabbalah, his heart opened. As it did, he became highly intuitive. He could look into a person's eyes and see their soul. A person can't be intuitive if his heart is closed. The Rav was not always open to new ideas but he was open to people. For all his scholarly knowledge, his astonishing insights often emanated from this quality.

The Rav had visions, however, they did not come to him as dreams. He saw them as fully realized. He saw them done. He had the idea of translating Rav's Ashlag's commentary on the Zohar and other kabbalistic texts into English, for instance. This was his vision. In 1973, after years spent compiling and editing, he published the second volume of the Study of the Ten Luminous Emanations. In 1974, he published An Entrance to the Zohar, a collection of Rav Ashlag's essays. The Rav's vision pointed the way, then he came in behind it to create a new reality.

* * *

In 1981, the Rav grew restless. We had hit a wall. We'd grown tremendously but it was difficult to make further progress in Israel due to the mounting influence of Orthodox Judaism. In the face of this swelling opposition, we found ourselves struggling. Despite having hundreds of students, we didn't have our own minyan or our own Torah

Scroll. We prayed in other synagogues because we couldn't establish our own. Our Sukkah was big enough for only eight or ten people to squeeze into.

In his compulsion to reveal more Light, the Rav decided to print the entire Zohar, a very expensive project—we're talking about 24 volumes. He thought he'd produce half of it and send it to the United States. Once we sold those books, we would print the other half. "It's never gonna happen that way, honey!" I told him. "If you really want the Kabbalah Centre to grow, we've got to establish a base. From there we can branch out. Why don't we go back to the United States? From there we'll create Kabbalah Centres all over the world."

"Nah, nah," was his immediate response.

"Let's do it," I insisted. Once again we were on the move. On the outside, my husband was tough like a Sabra but he listened and eventually he softened.

In December of 1981, we gathered our two young sons while Suri stayed behind in the Kibbutz, and pulled up stakes and moved back to New York. And we started again, climbing that next ladder.

CHAPTER 8:

MAKING IT IN NEW YORK

It would be nice to say that our lives became simpler once we returned to New York but that was not the case. Nevertheless, the Rav took the long view. "Chaos is not permanent," he would say, "because chaos only exists in the physical realm, the realm of illusion. Only Light is permanent." One of the things we learn in Kabbalah is that in this physical world, wherever there is Light there is an equal measure of darkness. We can't receive the Light directly, so we need to work for it. This is a spiritual law. The greater the intensity of Light, the greater the oppositional force.

Of course, my husband knew this, so he didn't see setbacks the way others might; they just encouraged him to proceed with even greater conviction. The Rav persevered when most of us would have given up. When we get hit by trouble, we don't appreciate that it is part of a system that was set up to help us win, not lose. Most of us don't have the commitment to rise above the distraction of what's going on right now to see the situation for what it really is. Instead, more often than not, we check out.

But the universe is set up in such a way that if we don't hang in there, the challenge becomes a missed opportunity. Difficulties are placed in front of us so that we can become the cause of the very Light we desire. Strength doesn't come from the Light. Courage doesn't come from the Light. Commitment doesn't come from the Light. These are qualities that arise within us. This is where our free will comes into play. In the Endless World, we, the Vessel asked the Creator to stay out unless we are the cause of letting Him in.

The Rav understood that obstructions are the *klipa*—the husk or shell that covers the Light. Something to be discarded or broken through so as to bring much more Light to the world. That's why he did not waver. And when those around him did, the Rav braced them. His certainty was contagious. "What it takes is awareness of the tools and certainty," the Rav would always say.

The Book of Exodus was the Rav's favorite illustration of certainty, one he turned to again and again. The Israelites, fleeing Pharaoh's army, arrived at the banks of the Red Sea. Faced with slaughter at the hands of the pursuing Egyptians or drowning, they prayed to the Creator for salvation. But in response to their pleas, the Creator responded, *Mah titzak elai*? "Why do you cry out to me?"

"Who should we cry out to, if not to God?" the Rav would ask, rhetorically. "God's reply meant that the Israelites should help themselves. They had all the tools they needed." The Rav lived by this tenet, and used it as a reminder to all the students of Kabbalah. "If we ever feel like crying out helplessly," he would bellow, "it is because we are not exercising what we have learned. There is not one single aspect of the physical reality that we cannot alter. For some of us, if change does not happen immediately, we lose our certainty. Do not let that happen."

It took the Rav twenty-one years to transform himself so that he could bring about the vision of sharing Kabbalah with the uninitiated world. Time had no meaning; those twenty-one years were but a day for him. "Do not ask, 'Why is it not happening now? How long will it take?'" he would say to his teachers. "If we are still asking, it will not work. These are the questions Satan puts in our mind. He will give every conceivable reason why things aren't working out the way we want them to. Don't listen. Kabbalah works."

For the Israelites, certainty meant walking into the Red Sea. Even when the water came up to their nostrils, they had to remain secure in the knowledge that the Creator did not take them out of Egypt just to see them perish. And so the Rav and I, too, waded in up to our nostrils with the same sense of inevitability.

* * *

We moved back to New York City. We rented a two-story, brick house on 72nd Avenue and Park Drive East in Kew Gardens Hills, a leafy bedroom community in the borough of Queens, right across the street from an off-ramp to the Van Wyck Expressway—the busy road to JFK Airport. It was a mere stone's throw from my mother's house on 77th Road. This was a neighborhood of comfortable attached homes. However, ours was a separate house on a corner lot, with a nice yard for the kids to play in. It was a far cry from our cramped walk-up in Brooklyn on Avenue N.

Over the next few years we moved and moved again, but we didn't stray far from this area. In fact, we bought the Centre's first house on my mother's street for $72,000, putting $10,000 down and taking a mortgage for the rest. Despite the fact that my mother and I had had a challenging relationship, we had some great years together in Kew Gardens Hills. It was nice for my children to live so close to their grandmother. And Suri eventually rejoined us.

The five of us were alone in Queens for about a year, which gave the Rav time and space to finish rewriting his first book, Kabbalah for the Layman. He had translated many books before but this was his initial foray into his own original work. He wrote an early draft in the 1970s while we were in Israel when he had long hours available. I thought it needed a major overhaul, so I encouraged him to start again. The rewrite was much better.

At that time we both worked from the home office we had set up in Queens, continuing one of the missions the Rav had started with Rav Brandwein—producing and distributing books on Kabbalah. I was calling people to ask if they were interested in buying the books of Rav Isaac Luria (the Ari) or Rav Ashlag's Study of the Ten Luminous Emanations. We sent books to universities, colleges, and various synagogues. We prepared invoices and receipts, and did our best to raise money to continue the sharing of this wisdom. The Rav spent long days studying and writing.

Since our main purpose in returning to New York was to teach Kabbalah to as many people as possible, the Rav asked a few of our Israeli teachers, young men with whom he'd had close relationships, to join us in Queens. It took a while for them to arrive. Eliyahu Yardeni was still in the army and couldn't leave for a year. A few of the other teachers had trouble obtaining visas. Others stayed in Israel to continue the Kabbalah programs and classes in Tel Aviv and Haifa.

Eliyahu was the first to make it to our shores in the winter of 1982. "I only think about Kabbalah," he told us excitedly the day he arrived. "No movies, no television, no music, just books of Kabbalah. I only want to talk about Kabbalah. There's nothing else in my head." I said, "Eliyahu! You have to be part of what's happening in the world." I decided to drive him to Manhattan and take him to visit museums. Of course, he didn't want to come; he only wanted to study and be with the Rav. The Rav turned to Eliyahu and said, "You must go. Consider it an order from me." And that was the end of that.

This was Eliyahu's first visit to America, no less New York, and he was overwhelmed by the huge buildings, honking cabdrivers, and hordes of rushing people on the streets. I still remember how a sign depicting the Big Apple confused him. "What is this apple?" he asked me. Today he laughs at his naivety. We visited museums together for a few days, and I tried my best to help him become more acculturated.

Eliyahu was an Israeli who had grown up in Paris. He joined the Israeli Army at the age of sixteen and was placed in a special course for young men who were having problems in school. Now, after years of study with the Rav, he had become a teacher and moved in with us. He slept in the same room as our sons, who were nine and ten at the time. They loved Eliyahu, who had often been their babysitter in Israel. Eliyahu was eager to begin the work he had come to New York to perform, and our first order of business was raising money to print books and to live.

The Rav and Eliyahu drove to the Williamsburg section of Brooklyn to meet with a man who could help connect us with people who enjoyed donating money to Jewish religious causes. This man was a driver for Orthodox men called *shlichim* (emissaries), who would come from Israel to collect money for various charities and yeshivas by knocking on doors. The generous donors they approached would spend a few minutes listening and then give something, sometimes $18, and sometimes more substantial gifts of $50 or $100. The driver was paid a percentage of their donations for his gas and effort.

Eliyahu had never done this kind of outreach before. In Israel we taught classes as a means to raise funds, and our students donated to our efforts. But as we had no students in New York, we needed to turn to this common method of raising money by going door-to-door. We called this *harisha*, which in Hebrew means "to plow."

The Rav and I were no strangers to the *harisha* practice ourselves. During the summers we would enroll the boys in sleep-away camp and travel around the United States fund-raising and selling books. The Rav loved to tell a story about one of our experiences on the road while we were engaging in harisha but he could never finish it without cracking up.

We would usually canvas in the religious community, which the *shlilchim*, the donation seekers from Israel, had already approached. One day, the Rav knocked on a door and heard the wife inside yelling at her husband. "Another one of those? Don't you give them a penny!"

The Rav could tell that this woman was accustomed to calling the shots in this household—in no uncertain terms. In that moment, this struck the Rav as very funny, so he started laughing. Suddenly the hen-pecked husband flung open the door. Surprised and embarrassed that he had been caught laughing at the man's misfortune, the Rav started pretending he was crying—that his large body shaking not with laughter but with tears.

The man, convinced that the Rav was sobbing, said, "Don't worry, don't worry. I promise I'll give you something!" as he ran into the house to fetch some money. (This was the point in his account when the Rav began laughing uncontrollably.) Not only did the Rav walk away with a few more dollars toward his goal of spreading the wisdom of Kabbalah, but he had a story that he never tired of telling.

Unlike the other *shlichim* in New York, Eliyahu wasn't satisfied with just receiving money. He also wanted to spread the wisdom of Kabbalah as he went from door to door. He came armed with books on Kabbalah, ready to teach. His passion was such that he would forget to eat breakfast. In fact, he wouldn't eat all day, so my husband began cooking breakfast for him.

I didn't like Eliyahu traveling alone since his English wasn't very good. I thought the Rav should accompany him but my husband didn't see it my way. "No. We must throw the baby into the water, and he will learn to swim. It's fine," he told me.

After two or three weeks, I still felt uneasy. I told the Rav, "Please find out more about what he's doing. He's out there representing us, and we need to know what he's saying." When the Rav inquired, Eliyahu told him that everyone who didn't believe in Kabbalah was a *klipa*, an empty husk; it was therefore their duty to contribute to revealing Light. This was nonsense. The Rav now understood why I was concerned. So he started driving Eliyahu and teaching him while they were alone in the car.

The Rav explained to Eliyahu what he had learned from Rav Brandwein when he was tasked with fundraising. When one collects *tzedakah* from someone, we provide that person with the opportunity to give for the purpose of sharing, which opens the flow of the Creator's Light. Eventually Eliyahu decided to close his eyes and not look at the amount a donor was giving him because he didn't want to judge. He just stuffed the money in his pocket—quarters or a dollar or two or a check—brought it to the bank, and trusted the teller to make the proper calculation. "We had no agenda beyond revealing Light," Eliyahu said after his education. "We were like Elijah the Prophet, knocking on doors and offering people the opportunity to give."

"I try to be truly poor," he would tell the Rav, meaning that everything he received was not to benefit himself but rather for the sake of giving a person the opportunity to share. The Rav taught Eliyahu a great deal on the subject and would later teach all the Chevre. The following comes from a transcription of one of those amazing talks:

> *If God is so loving and so full of abundance, why doesn't he take care of the poor? That's what some people ask. The answer is that God created all people for the benefit of those who have nothing. Poor people give those with money the opportunity to be able to give, and by their giving access a realm where there is no death. The technology of tzedakah kicks in.*
>
> *For a donation to be tzedakah, the recipient must be a poor person. Giving tzedakah to the poor is the only opportunity we have to sustain a life. When you study the Sefirot in Ten Luminous Emanations, you learn that this physical world is the world of Malchut, the world of matter that has no Light of its own. The channel that brings Light from the spiritual world to our world is Yesod. And the process of giving tzedakah mirrors the process of Light coming down to Malchut from Yesod.*

When tzedakah is given, the physical action creates the spiritual effect. By giving money to a poor person, we're actually opening up a channel of Yesod, which is the funnel of all Light for all the world, and that's how we draw the blessings to ourselves. The bigger the channel, the more Light that comes down to us and into the world. So that's the technical way that tzedakah works.

However, just performing the physical act of writing the check or putting the money in the hands of a poor man requires a consciousness to go with it. The more aware one is of what is taking place, the more Light that's revealed. Without the consciousness being activated, we don't get the same revelation of Light.

* * *

Eventually, other teachers, like Haggai Fridman and Shimon Sarfati, joined Eliyahu. We moved to a bigger house to accommodate everyone. The Rav and I slept in one room upstairs, our sons shared the second bedroom, and the Chevre had the run of the house downstairs. Every morning, after prayers and setting their consciousness, they took the subway to Brooklyn and Manhattan to do *harisha*. Rather than having someone drive them, they decided to walk from door to door in an attempt to interest people in Kabbalah and the books we had printed. At first they focused on predominantly Jewish communities: the Garment District in Manhattan, and Borough Park, Williamsburg, and Crown Heights in Brooklyn.

The money we made from sales and *tzedakah* was clothing and feeding all of us, as well as covering the cost of printing books. We were driven by our desire to provide more Kabbalah, more titles, more writings by the Ari, and more classes. We didn't have money for new clothing, so we shopped at thrift stores, looking for the warmest coats and suits we could find.

Our Israeli teachers were unprepared for New York's frigid winters. Sometimes they were so cold they couldn't speak; when a resident opened the door they could barely get a word out so the door shut in their faces. And, of course, summers were hot and sticky with humidity. The work was not easy.

I was a wife, a mother of four, and full-time administrator of the Kabbalah Centre's activities, as well as being responsible for all these young men. But we were on a mission the Rav and I, along with the "boys from Israel" as I called them, and our own kids. It was destiny in the making.

Residences in Manhattan and Brooklyn are mostly big apartment buildings. Many of these have doormen, guards, or locked security doors. It became a personal challenge for our young teachers to gain entry. Sometimes they would wait at the back door for a tenant to leave a building so they could sneak in. Then they would walk down the hallways knocking on doors until someone complained to the superintendent—which happened soon enough—and he would come looking for them. If they heard the super approaching, they'd run up or down a few flights of stairs and keep knocking on doors trying to talk to people. They did this until they were caught and told to leave.

Even when they gained ready entry, they were greeted with lots of push back and slammed doors. Non-Jews knew nothing about Kabbalah—for most, this was the first time they had ever even heard of it—and they were not interested. Slam! Non-religious Jews were familiar enough with Kabbalah to know that one had to be a rabbi over the age of forty to study it. Slam! But perhaps the most difficult crowd were the religious Jews.

My husband's reputation as a troublemaker had spread far and wide thanks to those who opposed him. The Rav was painted as a rebel and a heretic, a man who had deserted his many children for a younger wife who was a non-Jew. This group had already heard all they needed to know about my husband. Slam!

The teachers would come back to Queens every evening with new twists on the fanciful gossip, yet the Rav was unflappable. He would simply say, "Really? That's interesting. I don't even know these people." He was curious about what they were saying about him but he never criticized his detractors or complained about how uninformed they were. He just moved on as if these attacks had little to do with him, which they didn't. They were just temporary episodes with no significance in the larger scheme of things.

Despite the obstacles they faced, there were no gripes among the chevre. They knew they were fulfilling the vision to bring Kabbalah to everyone and change the world. They knew that someday everyone would be aware of Kabbalah because of their efforts. The Rav had predicted it with certainty, and they were confident that he was right.

As Eliyahu told me, "We never complained because there was nothing to complain about. If we didn't want to do this, we could always stop or go home. But nobody wanted to leave. We all loved the work, as tough as it was." After dinner, the Rav would go out with the teachers to one of the Jewish neighborhoods in Brooklyn or the Five Towns on Long Island to till the soil some more. People would be home for dinner, so there was a good chance to talk with them and reveal more Light.

Although the Chevre fixed themselves a light breakfast every morning, I fed them myself when they returned to Queens in the evening. Most of the time, a Kit Kat bar at midday was all that stood in the way of hunger. We all ate well on Shabbat, however. As we did not have our own minyan, we would often look for synagogues celebrating happy occasions like a Bar Mitzvah. In that case, there would be a Kiddush and lunch—challah and wine, a cholent (beef, potato, and barley stew) or gefilte fish or a deli platter—open to the whole community after the Shabbat services, and we would partake.

* * *

We all lived together under one roof. It was like a Kibbutz. For the first few years of our lives in New York, I didn't even have a key to that house in Queens. It belonged to everyone and there was always somebody in it. In fact, it literally didn't belong to me or the Rav. None of our houses did. They belonged to the Centre. We never owned any property in our names, nor do we today. Like the poor man, we had nothing of our own.

Although we were living together and had little money and no formal Centre, we all had the sense that we were generating Light, and that our lives were individually and collectively stronger and richer for it. The Rav reminded the Chevre not to worry about what others thought but rather to worry about their mission and the difference they came to make in people's lives. "You're a limited channel when you worry about what people think," he told them. "If you're dependent on their reaction, you're not dependent on the Light."

The Rav also counseled them that if they felt frustrated by rejection, they should approach their work with the consciousness that people truly need what we have to offer. He said, "If you're coming from that place, miracles will happen—people will open up." And over time that's exactly what happened.

After about a year of this dedicated activity, more and more people listened, bought books, and started to study. Some even asked for private lessons; they would read the books and then study with one of the young teachers. Some businessmen in Manhattan invited teachers to come to their offices. Students told their friends about Kabbalah, and the number of people learning increased, gradually but steadily.

We didn't have a dedicated location for the Centre yet, but people began coming to the house in Queens for the Rav's 5:00 AM classes on the Study of the Ten Luminous Emanations. He taught in the basement. Two or three of the men who attended were Chassidim, religious Jews who happened to be open-minded. Although they didn't divulge to their neighbors or friends that they were coming, they loved the wisdom. After the lesson concluded, the Rav would pray alone or with those who stayed until 9:00, 10:00, or 11:00 in the morning. And of course he would still arise in the middle of the night to study and learn, as he had always done.

Eventually, the Rav and I moved to an attached house and the Centre bought the one next door for the Chevre. Three young women arrived from Israel to work with us, and as fate would have it, they would marry three of our young men. The girls lived in the basement. In the mornings, they would go to Manhattan, set up tables on busy sidewalks, and sell the books and tapes of the Rav's lectures.

The extreme resistance we encountered at first eased up a bit. People were becoming reconciled to the fact that we existed. But there was still animosity for sure! Not only had the Rav left his family, but he also left a group unified by an identity that he no longer shared. The Rav always kept Shabbat and Kashrut—he never diverged from that path, though he did teach people who were neither affiliated nor Jewish. Some people simply couldn't accept that.

* * *

The Rav never stopped thinking about his children from his first marriage. They were still part of his life, even if he wasn't part of theirs. Many years later, our son Yehuda found a book at the Centre that the Rav had inscribed to the memory of Miriam Esther, the Rav's youngest daughter—the little girl who had died of leukemia at the age of three. My husband's grief was ongoing. Even though we were back in the United States, he still couldn't interact directly with his family, yet they were never far from his heart.

Then something miraculous happened. Naftali, the Rav's youngest son from his marriage to Rivka, the boy whom Rav Brandwein had blessed many years earlier in Israel, began to visit us. Naftali had had no contact with his father from the time he was about eight years old, though, after he heard that we'd returned to New York, things changed. He and the Rav went on walks together at a park in the city where they could talk. The Rav would ask him gently, "Why don't you come for a meal on Friday night? Please, come for Shabbat."

Naftali resisted. "I'll be honest with you," he told his father. "Shabbat is my one day off, and I prefer to do other things."

The Rav didn't demand that Naftali come but he persisted in his own firm yet gentle way. "It would be really nice to have you for Shabbat," he would say. "Don't worry about breaking the rule against driving. Just come. Just try to be here with me." Eventually Naftali did.

Slowly, the Rav reconnected with his son. He gave him a different explanation of the meaning of Shabbat and the prayers than what had been drilled into Naftali since childhood. The Rav taught him kabbalistic wisdom and showed him a different approach—one that Naftali could embrace.

The Rav explained something beautiful to Naftali that helped him understand why we do the things we do. The Rav said that Abraham the Patriarch saw in his *mazal*, his astrological chart, that he would not have a son. God took Abraham outside to observe the stars and told him to remove himself, to leave behind the cosmic influences of his astrological chart and raise himself *above* the stars. God said, "Look to the Heavens and count the stars. So shall be your children."

"From a metaphysical point of view," the Rav explained, "before the Revelation of the Bible on Mount Sinai, every creature of the Four Kingdoms—Human, Animal, Vegetable, and Inanimate—depended completely and solely upon the Zodiac and the planets. But with the Revelation on Mount Sinai, humanity was no longer subjected to the machinations of the cosmos."

The Revelation on Mount Sinai made it possible for humankind to change its destiny because the Bible and its precepts made it possible to connect with the cosmos in a way that allowed us to be the cause rather that the effect. The precepts are the channels we use to reach a level of consciousness by which we can become overseers of the planets and the stars. My husband said to his son, "There is free will as well as preordained destiny. Both can be possible."

The Revelation on Mount Sinai gave the Israelites then—and gives us today—the opportunity to raise ourselves above our astral influences. And Shabbat is one of the most powerful tools helping us become "determinators" of this physical world; the Rav coined this word, and used it all the time. It became part of the language he crafted to help us understand lofty concepts.

"Shabbat crowns all of the days of the week," he said, "because it combines everything into one unified whole, and we do not have to make an effort to connect with it. It was created with an all-inclusive harmonized energy-intelligence, without our intervention."

The Rav made clear that the word Shabbat does not mean a day of "abstinence from work." Rather, it means balance. "The Creator was actually very busy on the seventh day," the Rav would say, "gathering all of the differentiated thought energy-intelligence in the universe into one unified whole. This is an analogy for what we do on Shabbat."

It is only an illusion that the world is fragmented and that everyone is separate. Shabbat creates a force that gives us complete harmony. "When we keep the Sabbath," the Rav explained, "we create unity, peace of mind, and quietness. We are given a gift on this one day to make all of our connections, to refrain from anything that might create a distortion or fragmentation, not only within ourselves but within the cosmos. That's when we have achieved the Shabbat. That's what it's all about. So you see, it's not a precept that we are required to follow but one that we desire to observe."

After a few more of these discussions, Naftali started spending every Shabbat with us.

Two of his brothers didn"t want any contact with the Rav, and his other siblings weren't exactly thrilled that he was meeting with their father but Naftali became very much attached to the Rav and to our big extended family. Finally his older brother, Avraham, suggested that Naftali come live with us. "Naftali was not flourishing in the ultra-Orthodox community," Avraham told us. He had become rebellious and was getting into trouble. He had even stopped being observant. "Maybe you can help him," Avraham said. "Since we can't." We welcomed Naftali with open arms.

Naftali moved in downstairs with the other young men and lived with us for a while. He even tried knocking on doors for a few weeks but that wasn't his cup of tea. He did participate in other ways, though. He became involved in the storage, shipping, and handling of our books. He always saw himself as a working man rather than a scholar, so he became very active in developing the warehouse. He also helped out when the Rav gave classes. Eventually, Naftali heard from one of his sisters, "If this is what brings you back, then so be it."

Years later, after Naftali married, he and his family maintained a connection to the Rav and to all of our family. In the meantime, we were starting to get our feet under us. Our outreach was increasingly successful. We were printing and distributing books and holding classes. The Rav completed his second book, Wheels of a Soul, about reincarnation.

Even parts of the Rav's shattered first family were beginning to heal. And then, the unimaginable happened.

Once again, the universe provided my husband with fresh opportunities to earn the Light.

* * *

The Rav loved being in Israel. So once a year we traveled back to Tel Aviv. In the fall of 1983, we made our usual journey. When we arrived at the airport, some of the teachers who had stayed behind when we moved to New York were there to greet us. As soon as we saw them in the arrivals area, I noticed that they were wearing *tzitzit*, specially knotted, ritually fringed undergarments. They wore the fringes outside their clothes, as was the practice of ultra-Orthodox Jewish men. Rav Ashlag taught that they should be concealed.

"Uh-oh," I whispered to the Rav when I caught a glimpse of this. "We've got trouble." And sure enough, we did.

This was serious. Our trusted teachers were exhibiting symbols of Orthodoxy—precisely the mindset the Rav had rejected when he agreed to teach Kabbalah to religious as well as secular men *and* women. We decided that we couldn't return to New York after the holidays; instead we needed to stay in Israel and address this situation. We enrolled our sons in school and quickly rented a fifth floor apartment right outside Tel Aviv. We moved in, leaving our teachers in New York to temporarily continue the work without us.

The Rav could feel undertones of discontent among the teachers, so we decided to arrange a gathering with them to see what was on their minds. The Rav wanted to hear from them directly. Soon it became evident that many of our teachers had decided among themselves that the secular approach we had adopted wasn't for them. They had become interested in exploring the much more Orthodox approach to Kabbalah espoused by Rav Ashlag's grandson. He headed up a Yeshiva called Bnei Baruch and taught what he called the "deep Ten Luminous Emanations."

This was what they wanted to learn. They made it clear that they didn't have any negative intentions, and they told the Rav they didn't want to hurt him. They were just looking for something else. In our absence, the neighbor's grass had suddenly looked greener to them, and they were preparing to cross to the other side of the street.

I watched the color drain from the Rav's face. I was shocked. He was so upset that he had to leave the table and go to bed. I called a doctor fearing that he might have had a heart attack; that's how agitated he was. These were people who had lived with us for months at a time. They were excellent instructors. We trusted them, and they were family.

One by one our teachers began to abandon the Centre. The person who left first was a wonderful, charismatic educator. He and his wife, who was also a gifted instructor, moved away together. Until that point, they had led lives of dedication to Kabbalah as we taught it in the Centre. They had helped many people transform their lives, and now they were gone. Soon others drifted away too.

The Rav suffered. He accepted the departure of some of the teachers because he felt he had donc all he could for them. But others he felt he had failed. He mourned their loss and berated himself for not helping them enough.

In early 1984, we began making preparations for Purim. Rabbi Kahana, who had helped us so much over the years, arranged a *Beit Knesset*, a synagogue, for us to use for our Purim service because so many people wanted to attend. Purim is the one holiday in which Jewish people become inebriated for spiritual reasons. All of the teachers drank that night. My husband became quite drunk, so much so that he had to be escorted to the car. As he was getting into it, he saw one of our teachers. Although this teacher was still with us, the Rav started to cry—sobbing loudly, calling him by name. "Please don't leave me," he wept. "Don't leave me." He jumped out of the car and grabbed the man's hand. "Promise me you're not going to leave." Eventually, the others had to separate them because the Rav wouldn't let him go. It was heartbreaking.

The teacher was taken aback. "No, no. Of course I'm not going to leave," he said. "I have no intention of leaving." But two weeks later, he too was gone. Within a year, he passed away from cancer. Was this the reason the Rav hung on to him for dear life? Once again the Rav was left feeling he hadn't done enough to help this teacher.

Eventually, those who left took all of our books. They enticed students to follow them. One of our best teachers convinced 500 students to go with him. This, after they had said they did not want to harm the Rav, only to find a new path for themselves. It was devastating, and the Rav felt terribly hurt and betrayed. Only one teacher had chosen to remain.

The Rav took to bed for three days. We were both distraught. But at the end of those three days, my husband got up. "Okay, that's over with," he said, and he got back to work.

It took time to recuperate emotionally and to rebuild the Centre. At 58 years old, the Rav himself went back to teaching five nights a week. He couldn't cover what eight other people had, of course. I began teaching the "Introduction to Kabbalah." And we called on some of our instructors in New York to come back to Israel to help us rebuild.

I like to look back on our lives and see in them a progression. When the Rav's mother passed away, the Light sent him Rav Brandwein. When Rav Brandwein passed away, the Light sent me. In 1984, when so many key people walked away, the Light sent powerful new teachers to help us. Eventually they would become the most influential and dedicated leaders at the Centre.

My husband took the blame for the teachers' departure upon himself. In fact, one of the most interesting parts of this whole painful incident is that the Rav never once spoke ill of those who had abandoned our mission and undercut the survival of the Centre. He neither judged them nor acted vengefully. He recommitted himself to the mission of spreading the Light and Kabbalah rather than focusing on his personal feelings, and his sense of loss.

* * *

This wasn't the first time in my husband's life that he had to cut bait and move on. He did so with his first job as a teacher at the Yeshiva when he said, "This is not for me." Snip. He left behind his businesses and the world of politics to practice spirituality with his teacher. Snip. When his teacher died and he knew he had to make a change, he separated from his first wife and eight children. Snip. He had an amazing ability to look toward the future and deal with the hurts of the past. His vision was so strong and pure that he just kept on going, undeterred by distractions. He viewed them as temporary obstacles placed in his way that would eventually help him reveal more Light.

And we just kept moving forward.

APARCAR

CHAPTER 9:

BRINGING KABBALAH TO THE MASSES

The next two decades were extraordinarily eventful for the Rav, me, and the Centre. After being blocked at every turn for years, the Light of Kabbalah was breaking through. The Centre was no longer growing in a linear way, event by event. With his boundless energy, the Rav was moving things forward in many different directions and levels simultaneously. As our teachers fanned out around the globe and people started becoming aware of kabbalistic wisdom, their enthusiasm became palpable—you could literally feel it.

In addition to his myriad other duties, the Rav now spent countless hours on the phone—basically around the clock—teaching Chevre daily, working with them to shape their classes, helping them elevate their consciousness, guiding them through significant decisions, and coaching them on how to be caring teachers to their own students. In one dramatic instance in 2000, he supported our Chevre, Batsheva Zimmerman, just before she was being taken into the Colombian jungle to deliver the Rav's message of peace and the Zohar to the then leader of a paramilitary group and one of the most feared and dangerous men in the country. She was about to be driven blindfolded to a secret location in the jungle to meet him. Even the drug dealers escorting her were anxious. But the Rav wasn't, and he imbued Batsheva with certainty and strength.

"Remember," he told her softly on the phone before she embarked on this seemingly perilous mission, "Always remember the Light is with you. You're going to reveal the Light. The Light is protecting you." And she came through beautifully.

With 30 or 40 Chevre to teach, counsel and support, this was becoming an enormous job, but one the Rav relished because he knew he was fulfilling his teacher's prophecy. Often he slept only a few hours a night, but this didn't bother him. For the Rav, it was a question of purpose. He was spreading Light—and that's all that mattered to him.

It may have seemed to others that the involvement of celebrities triggered the Centre's enormous growth but from the Rav's view at ground zero, the expansion occurred as a result of all the excitement from our students and teachers. As they gained consciousness and insight they wanted to share Kabbalah with friends. And so we grew exponentially, each student inviting friends and family to classes, and those new students inviting their loved ones, and on and on it went. In this way, this next twenty-year span witnessed unprecedented progress in the spread of kabbalistic wisdom, which began to fulfill the Rav's most cherished vision.

The Centre didn't belong to us; it didn't belong to anyone. The Rav and I were merely the first volunteers. We were the original Chevre. The Rav was a pioneer who left his mark on history by making Kabbalah understandable and accessible to the masses. It was an unthinkable thing to do, yet he did it.

But I'm racing ahead of myself. Let's go back and pick up the thread of the story where we left off....

* * *

In 1984, after the Centre in Israel was up and running again, we headed back to New York. The Rav wanted our sons Yehuda and Michael to attend high school in the United States. He didn't believe in the Israeli system, in which students were practically slaves to certain institutions. Either they were totally religious and studied at yeshivas or they were totally secular and then joined the IDF, the Israeli Defense Forces (the army) immediately after graduation. There was no middle ground, which was not to his liking.

Back in the United States, the Rav and I picked up our lives where we'd so abruptly left off. We returned to the Kew Gardens Hills section of Queens but to a different house, and then we moved to the adjoining neighborhood of Kew Gardens, to a house at 124th Place. The Chevre still lived in Kew Gardens Hills, and could still walk to the new house. When another property came up for sale two doors down from us, the Centre bought it and the Chevre moved in there—so we were all very close together once again.

The Rav went back to teaching his 5:00 AM classes on Tuesdays and Thursdays and giving lectures, first in the basement of the house we lived in on 124th Place, and later in the house two doors down occupied by the Chevre. Occasionally, the Rav and I taught at the Gotham Book Mart, a famous bookstore and cultural landmark in Midtown Manhattan. I remember Holiday and Shabbat connections in that living room of the house on 124th Place. Our numbers were not always large but the energy and the love and the depth of every prayer was boundless.

One Friday night, after the services, the Rav and I, Yehuda and Michael, and a few of the Chevre were sitting around a ping pong table where we ate. The Rav wished each of us gathered around the table *l'chaim*—a toast to life. As his teacher had taught him, he used the toast of *l'chaim* to direct a special, individual message and blessing. We would practice this in all of our Centres between the fish and meat courses of the Friday night meal.

But on this particular evening, as he finished blessing those seated around the ping pong table, the Rav paused and said, "You know, there will come a day when each of you will be at a different Centre. We won't be together anymore." We all fell silent. On the one hand, it was painful to contemplate this kind of separation as the Chevre were so used to being in constant contact with the Rav. But on the other, this vision grew from the Rav's certainty, and it foretold the coming expansion of the Kabbalah Centre, eventually into far-flung places such as Russia, Brazil, South Africa, New Zealand, and the Philippines.

Of course, this tremendous growth didn't happen all at once. However, the Rav planted the seeds that evening in Queens. In fact, for some of the Chevre who were present, the Rav's words during this powerful Shabbat became a source of energy—a force driving us toward what was to come. These injections of consciousness put air under our wings. As small as we were, we felt huge; we knew that we were with the Light.

For most spiritual connections, Holidays, Shabbat, and Rosh Chodesh (the celebration of the New Moon, the beginning or "head" of each month), it was mostly our family and the Chevre and sometimes students joined us. Soon people would start to fly in from other cities to be part of Shabbat with the Rav. He would lead the service and at the same time teach the young Chevre how to conduct a Kabbalistic Shabbat. He would speak about the Bible portion before the reading to awaken consciousness and then again before each meal.

Over the years, as the numbers of students and interested people grew, it became pretty crowded in that house. So, despite the Rav's misgivings that we were overspending, the Centre bought what we now call the "big house" at 83-84 115th Street in Kew Gardens. It is a large two-story brick home with a semi-circular portico in front supported by four white columns. We taught classes there, and we used the house as a place to make spiritual connections; people would come in the mornings and stay for the whole day. Today it's referred to as the Kabbalah Centre in Queens.

Our lives never settled down into anything approaching normal. Most of the time, the Rav and I lived out loud and in public. We never had evenings where we said, "Tonight, let's just stay home as a family." We never took a family vacation. That was not our life.

In the new house we slept on the second floor, where there were two bedrooms and an extra room for the Rav's office. Yehuda and Michael studied there too. By this time, Suri had married and moved to Long Island with her husband. Downstairs, the house was devoted to Kabbalah. The kitchen and meeting rooms were communal spaces. Sometimes we would have up to 400 people in the house—a real crowd.

It was a *shtibl* (which literally means "small room" in Yiddish), a perfectly acceptable home synagogue of which there are many in Orthodox sections of New York today. The Rav was familiar with such an arrangement because he had experienced it as a younger man. Living this way was not uncommon, and it was what he had tacitly agreed to when he took on this role. That house was officially the very first Kabbalah Centre in the United States. But others were in the making.

* * *

The Rav began investigating other cities into which we could expand. He had sent Eliyahu Yardeni to scout out Los Angeles as early as 1983, and Eliyahu traveled between New York and Los Angeles several times. By 1985, he had rented a tiny guest house behind a larger home on Sycamore Street in the stately Hancock Park section, off La Brea Avenue in the heart of the city. The Rav wanted him to try teaching in this area, which had become an Orthodox enclave with yeshivas just around the corner.

Although Eliyahu's lodgings were extremely modest, the neighborhood was not. Sycamore is a tree-lined street of iconic Spanish-inspired homes and duplexes mostly built in the 1920s—the kind that Los Angeles is known for—with red tile roofs, arched French windows, and beautiful scroll-work wrought iron gates and grills. Eliyahu's apartment there was more like a converted garage.

Teaching there was not an option given its small size. So Eliyahu moved classes from one place to another, depending on where he could find a short-term, inexpensive space. Eventually, he found himself in a crisis. A man asked for his donation back and spoke badly about him. When he described this incident to the Rav during their daily conversation, the Rav said, "*Welcome to the world of Moses*," meaning that despite all he had done for them, the Israelites were always complaining to Moses and about him.

The Rav reminded Eliyahu, "Whatever happens to us in our lives provides spiritual opportunities for us to grow." But sensing that Eliyahu had hit a wall, the Rav suggested he return to New York for a few months. Eliyahu was not completely discouraged, however. He never is. After a short break he decided to return to Los Angeles, and he convinced the Rav to let him open a Centre there. With a lot of support from the universe that Centre did materialize, and in quite spectacular fashion. Here's how it unfolded.

Eliyahu had solicited donations every four or five months from a good-natured and successful businessman we'll call Joe to protect his privacy. Joe lived in Beverlywood, a relatively new but pleasant part of Los Angeles about three miles west of Hancock Park and just south of Beverly Hills. Joe gave small amounts, maybe $25 at a time. He was not interested in studying Kabbalah, yet on those rare occasions when Eliyahu found him at home, Joe was happy to make a donation and chat with Eliyahu about other things.

One night, quite unexpectedly, Joe and his wife showed up where Eliyahu was teaching. They came in with one of Eliyahu's students, who happened to be their friend. "She told us about the class she was taking, and it sounded intriguing," Joe said. Eager to learn more, Joe asked if Eliyahu gave private lessons, which of course, he did.

The following week, right after his first lesson, Joe told Eliyahu, "My wife and I have decided to start a Kabbalah Centre here in Los Angeles. I'll write you a check for whatever you need. Just give me a proposal." Fortunately we had created a similar proposal for someone else in Los Angeles several years earlier; Eliyahu just needed to update the numbers.

That same week, one of Eliyahu's friends told him about some office space for lease on Westwood Boulevard near Pico, less than three miles south of UCLA on the Westside of Los Angeles. It was on the second floor of a small strip mall, directly across from Junior's, a well-known local deli. Amazingly, this space was perfect for a fledgling Centre. It had been configured as a computer school but that lessee had just backed out of the deal. Eliyahu was delighted when he walked through the space. There was a big classroom, an office, and a waiting room. The walls had just been painted, and all the carpeting was brand new. What a Godsend.

Eliyahu called to tell us about this stroke of good fortune. "Okay, do it!" the Rav said, sharing in his student's excitement.

Eliyahu finished revising the proposal and presented it to Joe, who immediately wrote a check for a full year's rent. The Kabbalah Centre in Los Angeles was becoming a reality, assuming the rest of the pieces fell into place. One of Eliyahu's friends created an electric sign that read "Kabbalah Centre." They needed a permit from the city to mount it, which they quickly obtained, and the sign went up in a matter of days. Joe's business had many offices in Los Angeles, one of which had recently closed, so he had lots of extra furniture. "Come and take what you need—we've got couches, chairs, desks, and bookshelves," he told Eliyahu. Overnight, the Centre was fully furnished. After listening to a series of Kabbalah classes on tape, one student became so excited that he volunteered to step up and become chief cook and bottle-washer, taking care of all the odd jobs that needed doing. Now the Centre had a location and a staff!

The Rav decided there should be a Centre in Los Angeles, and it happened in a week! This soon became our business model. We put out the intention, set things in motion, and then followed opportunities as they emerged.

To share the teaching responsibilities, other teachers flew out to Los Angeles to help Eliyahu. During the day, they continued the *harisha* activities they had been performing in New York City, canvassing mainly in Jewish areas like the Fairfax district and some bedroom communities in the San Fernando Valley. They informed people that a new Kabbalah Centre was starting up in Los Angeles, and classes were available if they were interested.

Many people were still reluctant to hear our message, and some were downright hurtful. Still, interest and participation were growing on the West Coast, so the Rav and I started traveling to Los Angeles more frequently. He gave classes and lectures at the new Centre, and word began to spread.

* * *

While all of this was going on in California, by the late 1980s we also had Chevre flying to Toronto weekly to teach in modest spaces like the basement of a synagogue. Some committed Canadians jumped on the 45-minute flight to New York to join the Rav at the Big House in Kew Gardens for the intimate Shabbats we shared together. He and I began flying to Toronto three or four times a year with Yehuda and Michael to give lectures and introductory classes. In 1988, the Canadian government granted our request for status as a charitable religious organization.

One Shabbat in 1989, two hundred people attended the Rav's services and weekend lectures in Toronto. This was a tipping point: it had become clear that the Centre needed to buy a property in Toronto. One of our Canadian students, a real estate agent, brokered the deal for us. In Toronto, we opened communal meals and Holiday connections to all who were interested. And soon this Centre, too, began to grow.

Today, the Toronto Centre operates in a storefront. People take classes or attend services, and once they're exposed to the wisdom of Kabbalah, they want to be part of sharing it. This is how volunteering has become such an integral part of what we do at the Centre.

Back in West Los Angeles, despite a miraculously swift start, the Centre wasn't progressing as we'd hoped. The location on the second floor above a storefront was difficult to access from the street, and despite the electric sign, we were hidden away from people walking by. Moreover, the Centre was already becoming a victim of its own success. Though seemingly ideal at first, the space now felt small and crowded. As a consequence, new enrollment was slumping.

So the Rav and I returned to Los Angeles in 1990. When we got there, we scheduled a community meeting with the teachers and students. After listening to everything they had to say, I said, "Look, we're not growing because there's not enough room. Nothing's going to happen until we can address that issue. Either we move out of here into something bigger and better or we close the Centre."

This was shocking news but it led to a good result. The Rav and I spent a week or so in the city, and during that time a student of the Centre came to us with a suggestion. "You know, if you're looking for a larger space," he said, "I think I have the perfect spot."

"Okay, let's see it," I replied.

By now, we understood that we had a lot of requirements to meet. We needed to find a building that had a hotel nearby so people could come for Shabbat without having to worry about driving. The neighborhood had to be safe enough for people to walk around, even at night. This wasn't going to be easy. Then the student showed us a property for sale on Robertson Boulevard, right across the street from the Beverly Hills city limit. Half of it had been used as a community center and the other half as a Korean church.

I fell in love with it right away. It was a series of connected buildings, also in the traditional Spanish colonial style so prevalent in Los Angeles, with tiled roofs, archways, and an atrium, with flowers planted all around. The sanctuary, with its beautiful vaulted and timbered ceiling, was large enough to hold a crowd. There were spaces we could use as reception areas, meeting rooms, a book store, offices, and even rooms where we could create lodgings for ourselves and the Chevre. It was ideal!

But it also cost two and half million dollars. Real estate on the Westside of Los Angeles has always been very expensive, and this was no exception. Of course, the Centre didn't have two and half million cents, much less two and a half million dollars, but I didn't care. I told my husband, "We're going to buy this property."

Although the Rav had extraordinary clarity about spiritual things, and he had also been a successful businessman, he tended to be conservative, so in cases like this he would promptly freak out. "We shouldn't buy property for that kind of money when we don't have the cash in the bank," he insisted. "How are we going pay for it? We're going to go bankrupt."

"This isn't just a house in Queens," he continued. "It's a network of buildings that need a lot of work. I am not just worried about the down payment and monthly expenses; the buildings are falling apart. They need upgrades and repairs. Where's the cash going to come from? Also, there's no parking lot—a huge issue in a town where everyone has at least one car."

These were the Rav's concerns, and they made perfect sense. "Okay, let's see if it belongs to a private individual," I countered. "Maybe we won't have to put down so much money." This time, it was I who had the certainty. I remember saying to the Rav, "Listen, this is going to be a very big Centre, and it's going to do really well." By late 1990, some wealthy students got together to help us. After much back and forth with the real estate broker, the Centre bought the building on Robertson Boulevard, where it still thrives today.

I took charge of readying the place. I said to the Rav, "If you want to stay in New York, that's fine but I've got to live in California, at least for now. If you want to come, you're more than welcome. If you'd prefer to see to things in Queens, just come back to Los Angeles when the Centre is ready." The Rav stayed in Los Angeles.

I had bitten off quite a chunk. The buildings needed extensive work, since it had been designated an historic property, we couldn't touch the structure. This was a challenge because we couldn't leave it the way it was, either. I'm not just talking about cosmetic repairs; some fundamental issues had to be addressed. Luckily, I was able to fall back on my early experience with my first husband's construction business to navigate the hurdles.

The Centre was finally ready to open its doors in 1991. To inform the public, we advertised in newspapers in Los Angeles, we attended book fairs, and we placed large billboard ads in strategic spots. People began coming. Now, with Centres in New York and Los Angeles, Tel Aviv and Toronto established, we were travelling even more frequently, spending weeks at a time in each location.

The Rav focused his phenomenal energy on whatever Centre we were visiting, meeting individually with teachers and students, as well as presenting lectures to the local community. He was also on the phone, teaching and guiding the Chevre at all the other locations. And of course, he continued studying late at night and at quiet moments during the day. Yehuda and Michael were now older, so school was no longer an issue in terms of limiting our travels. If we were called on to be present to further the work of the Centre, the Rav and I were there.

* * *

Up to this point, our student base had been limited to mostly Jewish men and women. But I felt that Kabbalah couldn't change the world through spiritual study without *including* the world. Spiritual study for just one religious group felt too limiting for Kabbalah. We needed to become universal because the truth is universal.

I made this argument to the Rav, who agreed. So when we opened our doors in Los Angeles we pointedly welcomed anyone who had a desire to learn. As the Rav often used to say, "Wherever there's a vessel (the desire), that's where we'll be." This became our unwritten mission statement.

This shift to include the world-at-large had an unintended consequence, however. It led to the belief among Jewish people that we weren't Jewish or that Kabbalah isn't based on the Bible, which of course is not the case. I remember an incident when we first came to Los Angeles that said it all. One afternoon we were standing in line to order takeout sandwiches at a nearby kosher delicatessen on Pico Boulevard. Another deli patron, eyeing the Rav's beard and religious garb, asked him, "What do you do?"

The Rav replied, "We teach Kabbalah at the Kabbalah Centre."

So the man inquired, "Well, what exactly do you teach there?"

The Rav's response was to recite the words attributed to Rabbi Akiva and other great sages of different religions:

"'Love your fellow man as you do yourself. That which is odious unto you, do not do unto others."

The man's response, "Isn't that a Christian concept?"

The Rav was stunned. "No," he responded. "It's a principle that lies at the heart of every great religion."

Clearly, we had work to do. Yet we must have been doing something right because attendance kept growing.

* * *

At our first major event at the Los Angeles Kabbalah Centre, I gave an introduction and the Rav presented a lecture. The Centre drew 500 people that evening, which was more than we'd ever seen in one place before, including New York, Tel Aviv, and Toronto. Soon we had 350 members—another record. Then celebrities started to show up unannounced and without fanfare, often invited by students who were their friends and wanted to share this wisdom with them. Before long, a number of pop culture icons had become associated with the Centre, placing it squarely in the public eye.

The Rav was unaffected. To him, celebrities were people just like anyone else, struggling to find answers and Light. Interestingly, the Rav was also not surprised by the Hollywood connection. He had always believed that our message to the world would come through Hollywood. "The west is where the sun sets," he would say. "According to the Study of the Ten Luminous Emanations, that makes it the receiver, Malchut. This is why we are in Los Angeles. Because it's where the Light gets manifested."

The opening of the new Los Angeles Centre was pivotal to us as an organization. In the past, we had been more or less flying by the seat of our pants. However, the spacious complex on Robertson Boulevard and a large local community meant that our growth forced us to create a more defined corporate infrastructure for our spiritual organization. We were in a new world in which we were required to deal with lawyers and accountants and a board of directors. The Rav would say, "The blessings come from being *asuk baTorah*—being busy with the Torah," which means treating the spiritual work as if it was your business, and we were. Very busy.

And even though the Rav had warned me, "It can't be done. It can't be done," the Los Angeles Centre paid off its mortgage in three years. It was fast. Lightning fast.

* * *

Inspired by his love for all humanity, the Rav embarked on many different projects during these years of startling growth. I've already mentioned our mission to distribute Zohars in New York after the horrific attacks on September 11. Another undertaking that took hold around this time and which occupied the Rav for the better part of a decade was Kabbalah Water.

The unique chemical properties of water had always intrigued the Rav. Water has the ability to dissolve many other substances; its solid form, ice, is *less* dense than its liquid form; its boiling point, viscosity, and surface tension are all unusually high for its molecular weight. Water is indestructible, yet also mutable. When you sip a glass of water, you're swallowing a three-billion-year-old liquid. Unlike milk that will sour in a matter of days, it never spoils. Water has other mysterious properties that make it one of the most unusual compounds in the universe—and of course nothing we know of can live without it. Water is the crucial element that NASA scientists search for when they're looking for signs of extraterrestrial life.

Water also possesses profound spiritual properties. The Zohar says water is the closest substance on Earth to the Light that radiates from the Creator. The Zohar explains that the universe was shaped by the consciousness of mercy that is inherent in water—the energy-intelligence of sharing (*chesed*). The Zohar says that *chesed* is also the power of *echad* (one). *Chesed* is our unified state. According to the Rav, "As a result of humanity's negative actions at the time of Noah, however, water developed a secondary nature. It became a force that could also harm in the form of tsunamis, hail storms, blizzards, or floods." He went on to say, "Our problems stem from the fact that we have left behind the consciousness of *echad* (one)." The Rav believed that if we experienced the true nature of water, we could reconnect with the consciousness of unity.

The late Masaru Emoto, a Japanese author, researcher, and homeopath said that human consciousness can reconfigure the molecular structure of water. Emoto believed that water could react to thoughts and words both negative and positive, and that polluted water could be cleaned through prayer and positive visualization. In the late 1990s, he published several volumes of a work entitled *Messages from Water*, which contain photographs of differently shaped ice crystals formed when scraps of paper with messages were placed in or near vessels filled with water.

The Rav's kabbalistic beliefs about water were much like those of a physicist. For decades, he sought ways to restore water to its original unified form. Beginning in the late 80s early 90s, he experimented with electricity to find a way to charge water and awaken its dormant nature. He placed water nearby when he prayed and studied, trying different ways to load it with spiritual energy.

The Rav found an aquifer in Canada with remarkably pure spring water. The Centre bottled this water and put cases of it in our synagogue to infuse it with spiritual energy from prayers and the Bible. He also brought a committed group of positive-minded people to the warehouse where we stored the water. There, they meditated and prayed using sequences of the 72 Names of God to create what we call Kabbalah Water, which we sell in individual bottles.

But the Rav, as usual, had larger ambitions. The 1986 nuclear disaster at Chernobyl disturbed the Rav deeply. He decided to use Kabbalah Water to neutralize the nuclear fallout in the region's polluted lakes. Remember the Rav's statement that, "When you bring Light to bear on the darkness, the darkness goes away"? Well, water is Light and nuclear damage is darkness, so the Rav got to work. He came up with a plan to grow plants using Kabbalah Water, which could be planted around these polluted lakes. He also worked with doctors and scientists to establish how much Kabbalah Water it would take to clean the lakes if the water was poured into them directly.

This was a noble undertaking, for sure. The Rav wanted to make a major contribution to global healing. However, I didn't join his nuclear energy project because I thought it was too lofty. My idea of healing the world was to start small, with individuals, and then go outward from there, one person at a time. I believed Kabbalah Water should be used to help people, not to clean up nuclear accidents. We argued. This time we didn't come out on the same page. It was the only project we didn't work on together. And despite his heroic efforts, to the Rav's great frustration, the global goals he envisioned from the Chernobyl undertaking did not manifest to the level of his satisfaction.

* * *

Although the Rav hit a wall with the water project, he did find great success in spreading the wisdom of Kabbalah elsewhere. In the late '80s, the Rav had the foresight to begin sending Chevre to other countries to teach and do outreach for a few weeks or even a few months at a time. They traveled in pairs or groups of three. They went to Mexico. Then to England—to London, Manchester, and Leeds. In London it was easier for us to establish a Centre because the language didn't pose an obstacle.

One day, a man called the Rav in New York and begged him to bring Kabbalah to London. He had had a dream about the Rav. He would give the teachers who would come a house, a car—everything they needed to start doing the work of teaching Kabbalah! That was the seed, and it quickly bore fruit.

The Rav sent Chevre to feel things out in Brussels and Antwerp in Belgium. Others traveled to South America—to Buenos Aires, Argentina; Montevideo, Uruguay; and Rio de Janeiro and Sao Paulo in Brazil. Often, they went to a particular city because one of our students lived there and invited us with a promise to accommodate the teachers we sent. The circle kept growing.

Around 1995, the Centre bought a 40,000 square foot building in Tel Aviv on Dizingoff Square. Although it was old and neglected, it was situated right in the most vibrant part of the city. We refurbished it and established a Kabbalah Centre there but it wasn't thriving. Upset by the lack of progress he saw on subsequent trips to Israel, the Rav called one of our teachers in New York and asked if he could move to Tel Aviv to take over managing that Centre.

"Yes! Sure!" he said, "I'll pack, put some things in storage, and I'll get there by next week."

But the Rav was in a hurry. "Can't you come earlier?" he asked.

"Earlier? When? Tomorrow?"

"No," the Rav responded. "Today. Move today."

Ordinarily the Rav was a big believer in patience and for the most part, he moved slowly when it came to major decisions. I was the one who liked to jump. But in this case, there was a reason the Rav was so eager to finally get a Centre firmly established in Israel. He believed that Israel is the spiritual center of the world, so whatever happens has a global ripple effect. He had been patient for years but now he could wait no longer.

That very night, the Chevre flew from Los Angeles to Israel and took over the Tel Aviv Centre. As if responding to the Rav's sense of urgency, the Centre revived and began to bloom. For the Rav, Tel Aviv would always be one of the most important Centres.

* * *

In 2001, during one of our many trips to Israel, the Rav became involved in the political hot potato known to the world as the Israeli-Palestinian conflict. Israel was engaged in constant on-again, off-again hostilities with the Palestinians, responding with military force to terrorist attacks, bombings, and other deadly provocations. A blueprint for peace had been laid out in the Oslo Accords signed in 1993 by the Israeli Prime Minister, Yizhak Rabin; Yasser Arafat, leader of the PLO; and President Bill Clinton. However, despite the fact that Rabin, Arafat, and Israeli Foreign Minister Shimon Peres had received the Nobel Peace Prize for crafting this agreement, a true peace in the region has not been achieved.

The Rav, like Rav Ashlag and Rav Brandwein before him, understood that although Kabbalah was a spiritual pursuit and should not be intermingled in politics, creating harmony in this region would provide an energetic catalyst to world peace. So, like his teachers, he spared no effort in meeting with political leaders to help awaken a higher consciousness as they made decisions. The Rav saw political involvement not as a secular enterprise but as an extension of his spiritual mission to spread Kabbalah and reveal the Lightforce of the Creator.

During this particular visit, with the help of students in the Centre who had political contacts, the Rav reached out to both the sitting Israeli Prime Minister Ariel Sharon and to Yasser Arafat. He started separate conversations with the two men, while also making each one aware that he had a connection to the other and could serve as a conduit if needed. Sharon had been a general in the Israeli Defense Forces, participating in almost all of Israel's wars. As a military man Sharon had been bellicose but as Prime Minister, he had become more pragmatic and open to the possibility of peaceful options. However, many of the government officials in his orbit did not feel as he did. Sharon shared this dilemma with the Rav and began using my husband as a sounding board for his new ideas.

The Rav's discussions with Yasser Arafat centered on that leader's internal struggle. Arafat was also a man who knew how to fight, what he didn't know was how *not* to fight. Arafat trusted the Rav and told him that his sense of purpose was tied up in his people's struggle against Israel. The Oslo Accords had put him in a position where he had to let go of that past, and so far he hadn't been able to do so.

This was making it almost impossible for the Palestinians to reach a permanent agreement with the Israelis.

The Rav's influence culminated during a siege on Arafat's residence in the city of Ramallah. The British had constructed a series of buildings across the Palestinian territories when they occupied the area in the 1920s. Built of white Jerusalem stone, they served as forts, offices, residences, police stations, courts, and prisons, and they became known as the Mukata'a, or headquarters. As a result of the Oslo Accords, the Palestinian Liberation Organization (PLO) took over these structures, and Arafat moved into the Mukata'a in Ramallah in 1996, when it became the official headquarters of the West Bank administration.

In the spring of 2002, the Israel Defense Forces began laying siege to some of these Mukata'a in an effort to put an end to terrorist attacks. The Mukata'a in Hebron, for instance, was totally destroyed. Others were partially demolished. In June of that year, after a devastating suicide bombing in Tel Aviv, the Israeli Defense Forces (IDF) attacked the Mukata'a in Ramallah, intending to use tanks and bulldozers to raze the compound.

At this dire time, unbeknownst to the world at large, Arafat asked the Rav to intervene with Sharon. "They are killing us here," he said. Although the two leaders were officially not communicating with each other, the Rav, acting as a go-between, effectuated a bit of movement. He was able to get them both on a conference call. The IDF stopped its bulldozers from destroying Arafat's compound. However, Arafat was left inside in a stalemate that would last for the next few years. During the slow-motion Israeli-Palestinian conflict the temperature goes up and down. My husband became involved at a moment when the situation had become really hot, and he was able to lower the intensity a bit.

* * *

This wasn't the only time the Rav intervened and brought the Light of Kabbalah to world affairs. More than a decade earlier, in 1989, again through one of our students, the Rav had developed a relationship with King Hassan II of Morocco, father of the current King Mohammed VI. This student, who was close to both King Hassan II and the Rav, asked the Rav to come to Morocco as the guest of the King. Some serious problems were afoot, and King Hassan was nervous. This was more than ten years before the 9/11 attack; even then, radical Islamists were creating unrest around Morocco, and threatening to take control of the country.

The Rav and I flew from New York to Morocco's capital, Rabat, hauling boxes of the Zohar along with our luggage. The King provided us with a private plane so we could travel around the country to pray for peace and distribute these holy books. We spent a week distributing Zohars all over the kingdom while the Rav studied and prayed in every town we visited to anchor that spiritual energy. We left the Zohars with Muslims and Jews who would continue the study or keep the books in their houses as blessings. During our journey, we also visited the graves of Moroccan kabbalists, and the Rav prayed there too. Eventually, Morocco's internal troubles subsided.

The presence of kabbalists in Morocco may be surprising given that this is an Islamic nation. However, after the expulsion of the Jews from Spain in 1492, a group of kabbalists sailed across the Mediterranean and arrived in North Africa, settling in areas now known as Algeria, Morocco, and Tunisia. Over time, hundreds of thousands of Jewish immigrants left Morocco for safer places like France and Israel, however in Morocco one can still find the resting places of kabbalists if you know where to look for them.

After that week of travel, we met with King Hassan II several times in his palace. It was a magnificent structure, with an enormous entry framed by columns and traditional horseshoe-shaped arches. One of the remarkable things that the King shared with the Rav was a parchment with the 72 Names of God written on it. It had been passed down in his family for generations. When King Hassan's father had given it to him, he said, "Make sure you keep this under your pillow at night. It will protect you." The King wanted to understand the significance of this parchment covered in Hebrew letters, and the Rav was only too happy to oblige.

The Rav and the King developed a warm friendship, which continued for many years thereafter. They met annually when the King invited my husband and I to the Fezevun (Feast of the Throne), a celebration of the day the King had ascended to his position. There were private gatherings that day within the palace, which the Rav attended. When the first Gulf War was brewing in 1990 and Saddam Hussein was threatening to invade Kuwait, the Rav jumped on the phone with King Hassan and suggested, "Let's try to call Hussein together." The Rav was hoping the conflict could be averted or at least resolved without bloodshed. In a last-ditch effort, the Rav asked the King to make one more attempt at peace before committing his troops to the fight against Iraq.

King Hassan made the call but unfortunately for the world, Hussein did not respond, and the opportunity was lost.

* * *

During these years, the Rav moved constantly, going wherever he was summoned, despite the danger. In 1992, a group of 200 students studying in Caracas, Venezuela invited the Rav to give a lecture and celebrate Shabbat with them. It was an opportunity to reveal Light in a country that desperately needed it, so he jumped at the chance. We flew there with Yehuda, Michael, and a Torah Scroll, and stayed at the Eurobuilding Hotel, a large modern structure directly across the street from La Carlota, the Military Airport.

Unbeknownst to us, Lieutenant Colonel Hugo Chavez had organized a coup that was to begin the very next morning. We woke to the din of machine gun fire, and from our hotel windows we could see tanks rumbling along the street and into the air base. The rebels had seized key communications and military installations throughout the city, including the presidential residence and the defense ministry. Their goal was to capture and kill President Carlos Andres Perez.

We were urged by hotel staff to stay away from the windows and to crawl under our beds for safety as planes flew overhead, dropping bombs. A strict curfew was imposed, and although Shabbat was approaching, we couldn't leave the hotel. In a situation reminiscent of the Yom Kippur Neilah prayers in Jerusalem so many years earlier, the Rav decided to conduct the Shabbat service in a small room in the hotel and invited anyone who wanted to join us. By Sunday, things had calmed down enough so the Rav could give a well-timed seminar on the illusion of chaos.

In the end, the coup was foiled, the president managed to flee the scene, and Hugo Chavez was taken to prison. Tragically, 143 people were killed. Two years later, Chavez was freed from prison, and he would become Venezuela's elected president in 1998.

* * *

Along with his own efforts on behalf of peace, the Rav also encouraged the Chevre scattered around the globe to help leaders find paths to conflict resolution. Troubled by the intractable bloodshed in Colombia, in 2000 the Rav sent one of the Chevre, Batsheva Zimmerman, to give Zohars to the country's president, his predecessor, and other government officials. Through a series of contacts, Batsheva was able to reach these leaders and hand out the Zohars.

While in Bogota, at the Rav's request, Batsheva also met with the head of a paramilitary group and his two foes, the kingpin of FARC (Revolutionary Armed Forces of Colombia) and chief of the ELN (National Liberation Army), who was in prison at the time. Batsheva even went to see the boss of the Cali drug cartel. To all of these men she delivered Kabbalah books and the Rav's message. "The Rav wants you to know that you cannot remove darkness using more darkness. Only Light will take away the darkness."

Over time, the effect of the Rav's words and the wisdom of Kabbalah on these individuals was transformative. In 2001, Pacho Galan, the chief of the ELN, sent Batsheva a note thanking her and the Rav for the Zohar.

> *My dear Batsheva:*
>
> *Here I am facing the Universe, in the presence of Rav Berg, concentrated in the Heart of my country invoking that the Light becomes Peace, and we can live eternally as brothers. I join with all my energy to this universal human scale of which at this moment we are concentrating in the Zohar, dreaming and building a better world for all. My country is at war, it needs peace. My country is wounded, it needs healing. My country is*

in darkness, it needs the Light. My country suffers, it needs consolation. [...] I embrace Rav Berg and you, and together in a single Ray of Light we light the bonfire of Peace for Colombia and the World!!!

By 2010 Pacho started to actively seek peace among all the groups, organizing face-to-face meetings of the leaders of FARC, ELN, and the paramilitary. Sitting down with former mortal enemies, these men worked to create a bridge to peace and forgiveness in Colombia.

Before leaving Colombia for prison in the United States, the leader of the Cali cartel also sought to change his ways. He asked for forgiveness for the damage that he had done to Colombia. The head of the police told Batsheva, "We didn't understand what happened to him, but I understand now. You taught him Kabbalah. He has the Zohar, so now we understand why he changed."

Why approach these dangerous individuals? The Rav would ask, "Why not?" He didn't judge people. He had no enemies save those opposed to the dissemination of Kabbalah. He was concerned for the wellbeing of all, even those who engaged in violence. As for fear, it didn't affect the Rav. He believed he could walk unscathed through the eye of a storm, and he was so full of love for humanity and purpose that nothing touched him.

When Batsheva asked the Rav why these people had changed so much and were now seeking peace, he said, "When we speak to them, we speak to their souls. And of course, all of their souls are looking for the same thing. But there is the ego, the dark force that plays with everyone. That's why it's so important to continue this work. If they have Light consciousness, you can imagine what they can do, not just for their country but also for the world."

* * *

In 1995, at around the same time the Centre bought the building in Tel Aviv, we also turned our attention back to New York. There, we found a narrow but deep property wedged between two other buildings on East 48th Street, between Lexington Avenue and Third Avenue in Midtown Manhattan, right around the corner from the Waldorf Astoria. This would become the New York Kabbalah Centre headquarters.

Like the project in Los Angeles, it was no small undertaking. The interior had to be gutted and rebuilt from scratch. We decided that it would be more economical if we worked directly with subcontractors instead of engaging a general contractor. Once again, I took on that role. We sent out for bids and subcontracted the entire reconstruction. It's a lucky thing we did because we changed the plans ten times over, and we didn't finish the renovation until 2000!

The Rav made me crazy! He'd say, "You don't know what you're doing." Today, the building has a dignified façade, and inside there are classrooms, meeting rooms for one-on-one counseling, offices, a bookstore, elevators, and a space for our spiritual connections and events.

We've created an amazing community there, with more than a thousand members. Now our message was catching fire in New York as well as Los Angeles and Tel Aviv. We were truly on our way!

CHAPTER 10:

TRANSITIONS: THE DECADE THAT CHANGED THE WORLD

In the nearly fourteen years that began with Y2K hysteria and ended with the Rav's passing, a series of events brought calamity and progress to the world. In the year 2000 (5760 in the Lunar calendar), an unusual cosmic shift took place. First a little background. The number 5760 reflects the quantity of *se'ah* (the amount of water used to fill a *mikvah*). *Se'ah* is an ancient unit of weight measurement equal to the amount of liquid held in an egg. As you recall, the *mikvah* is a ritual purification bath used for spiritual immersion. According to Rav Ashlag, while a person is immersed in this body of water, they are freed from any aspect of negativity, and death itself cannot attach to them. The Rav inferred from this that the year 5760 marked the opening of an age when the Angel of Death would lose his hold on humankind, and immortality would become achievable.

That year, the Centre hosted a Rosh Hashanah event that drew almost 3,000 people from everywhere in the world. We'd never assembled such a large and diverse crowd before.

In his lecture during the holiday service, the Rav told the congregation that the 17th century Kabbalist Rav Avraham Azulai, had predicted that with the onset of the year 5760 in the Hebrew Calendar, the Light of Immortality would begin its descent to this world. However, he also made it clear that Satan would not leave without a fight. This decade revealed to us both the greatness of our battles won and the tenacity of chaos's final efforts to convince us otherwise.

In many ways, these years did bring with them technologies that would lead to the removal of space between people, and the exercise of some control over the Angel of Death. In ways unimaginable to past generations, technology was helping to unite all the sparks of the Vessel, eliminating the barriers of time, space, and motion. Medicine was discovering ways to eradicate genetically based disorders and create an environment receptive to eternal life. Information and connectivity proliferated as never before. And the battle against the force of death became fashionable to half a billion people in the form of a young fictional wizard, whose virtues would help good triumph over evil.

On September 11, 2001, however, tragedy struck when 2,977 people died as a result of terrorist acts in New York and Washington. The event also created unity among nations, a global gathering to focus on what unites us. At least for a short time.

The soil was ripe for the seeds of immortality to take root.

Then, on September 2, 2004, my husband had a devastating stroke. For a long time I didn't know what to do. We had always participated in everything together, and now for the first time since I was twenty-something, the Rav was not continually by my side. He had taught me that everything happens for a reason, it is all part of a spiritual system that pushes us to become who we need to be. So I asked the Creator, "What do you want my husband's stroke to teach me? What do you want me to do now?"

That stroke was a defining moment in our lives. After the initial trauma faded, I stepped out from behind the Rav, as we all did. His presence, like that of a great redwood tree, had made it difficult for others to grow in his shadow but now we had no choice. Now that the Rav had reduced himself, we all found room to develop in ways we had never considered when he was at full capacity. I began to take on a more independent role and assumed some of the traveling, writing, and speaking. Yehuda and Michael also stepped in to fill the gap. They started writing books, traveling, and teaching, as well as working with the Chevre while also taking on their own projects. So, rather than collapsing, the Centre kept on growing despite the Rav's impairment. Perhaps this was the Creator's plan all along.

It took time for me to regain my footing and move forward, but with the benefit of hindsight, I understood the choice the Rav had made. Much as I missed his physical involvement, I do believe the stroke was a choice. Knowledge of the spiritual nature of things helps a great deal in working through the circumstances that life presents.

It helps us to worry less. It's funny how we become stressed about events, and yet we know that in the end it will all work out just as it was meant to. If we could only remember that.

In a letter to the Rav, his teacher Rav Brandwein wrote something that relates to this idea.

> *I heard that you are very worried that things are not working out properly. My opinion is that you should not worry so much about physical things since they do not last forever. It would be better if all your concern be concentrated on spiritual matters as they are eternal and that you fulfill the aspect of "behold, the Creator is my salvation, I will trust and be not afraid."*

It took some time, but I developed greater and greater strength. My biggest fear has always been to be alone, and now I had to choose to grow and feel the Creator's presence near me in a different way. Now I was able to do many things I couldn't do before. The Rav's stroke triggered my own transformation. As if to underscore that point, the Rav kept pushing me away. At first, I was hurt by this. Then confused. But finally I began to suspect he was doing it for my own good.

This was confirmed by a conversation the Rav had with a friend shortly before the Rav left this world. As he looked at a picture of the two of us, the Rav said, "People wonder why I am so hard on Karen. I must be, so that she will not stay with me. Her job is to go out and do what she came here to do. And when she is done, we will be together again."

* * *

There were inklings; there were signs.

A year before the stroke, Michael had the sense that the Rav was talking about life in a different way, depending on and trusting him to an unusual degree. The quality of their relationship had changed, and Michael was trying to understand why.

On a Shabbat lecture in August, several weeks before the stroke, the Rav challenged the gathered visitors, students, and Chevre in a way I'd never seen before. "Why are you coming to the Rav with your questions? I have given you all the tools I have so that you can become the Rav for yourselves. Now you become the Rav!" His vehemence and his words stunned us all. In the Zohar, Rav Shimon says each and every one of us has the potential to become Rav Shimon. But what could the Rav's words have meant to the congregation at that moment? Everyone was puzzled.

Then again, on August 28th 2004, the Shabbat before the stroke, the Rav gave us another clue in his talk from the pulpit. It was as if he had foreseen what was about to befall us, and he wanted us to be prepared.

> *When things get tough, when everyone else will say it can't be done, where will you be? Will you remember the difference between you and*

everyone else? All you have to say is "It's an illusion, I can control it." You know why? Because you have captured the energy of this portion. There is a guarantee of the removal of chaos. And when the test happens, and this is what life is all about, "zachor," remember it's only a test. It means it's a false alarm. The alarm goes off, "Fire," but in comes a voice that says, "It's only a test."

It is a simple idea, it's only a test, do not be ashamed, do not be afraid to say, "No, no, I will not accept it."

This is where the Satan is still left with the only remaining tool, to create uncertainty. In this day, in the time of Aquarius, for Satan it's all over. His last resource is to create an environment to make us forget that we are in control.

There were physical signs too. A few days before the stroke, while he was sitting in our backyard, the Rav said, "Yesterday, I had a terrible, terrible headache. It was so bad…" then his voice trailed off. We had never heard him speak this way before. Was this also a way of preparing us?

* * *

The Rav didn't believe in Western medicine and, like his teacher, he often refused to take it. For instance, during a trip to Paris, the Rav had a bout of cellulitis—swelling in his leg due to a bacterial skin infection. A doctor there gave him an antibiotic, and he soon recovered. A few years later, the cellulitis returned while we were home in Los Angeles.

"I don't want to take medicine," he told me.

Sometimes, I didn't have the strength to argue with him, so I said, "Okay." The first two days, he got by without antibiotics. On the third day, I took him to the hospital with a raging infection and a temperature of 104. After I stopped worrying, I was peeved. Once his temperature had returned to normal, I sat by the side of his hospital bed and asked him, "Is this better than taking the antibiotic?"

In March of 2004, six months prior to the stroke, the Rav had seen an internist because he was experiencing heart palpitations. The doctor said, "Listen, you have atrial fibrillation, which means the two upper chambers of your heart aren't pumping normally. They're beating too fast and sometimes twitching chaotically. This is not a life-threatening condition but it can lead to complications like strokes, which *are* life-threatening."

There are ways to regularize the heartbeat, like inserting a pacemaker. There are also blood thinners like Coumadin that help prevent clots from forming in the first place. The doctor was pretty blunt about it. He said to my husband, "Either you take a blood thinner or you're going to have a stroke." This may sound straightforward but we're talking about Rav here. He refused the medications.

"I believe alternative medicine is the way to go," he told me. So we argued.

"Okay," I said, "believe anything you want, but you're going to take the Coumadin!"

He refused. And that was that.

Six months later we were in a beautiful Las Vegas hotel with our son-in-law, who was launching a new line of clothing at a trade show there. When we came back to our room following the reception that Thursday night, the Rav started to complain of abdominal pain. I called a doctor. When I told him the Rav's age, he refused to come because the Rav was a Medicare patient.

"I don't care about Medicare," I told this physician. "I'll pay you privately."

"That's illegal," he said to me and hung up. I called a friend who was a doctor and said, "The Rav is having some kind of stomach problem. I don't know what it is." He suggested I give him a strong painkiller, and the doctor called in a prescription. Once the Rav took the pill, he felt better and slept. The next morning, his condition seemed to have improved.

Nevertheless, I had a feeling we needed to return to Los Angeles pronto, so I left the Rav in the care of our assistant, a young woman who had accompanied us to Vegas, and went down to the lobby to check out. When I returned not ten minutes later, the assistant said, "Something's wrong with the Rav. He's in the bathroom, and he's talking strangely." I ran to the bathroom and found the Rav burning up with fever and wracked with pain. Because of our past experience with high temperatures, his ramblings didn't surprise me. But this time seemed different.

"Call 911," I shouted to her. I thought the Rav was having an attack of pancreatitis. The ambulance came quickly, but we ended up driving around Las Vegas for an hour because the hospitals were full, and the medics couldn't find an ER that would take him. As frightening and frustrating as it was for me, this too must have been part of the Creator's plan.

While I was in the back of the ambulance with its sirens wailing, I was able to make out alarms going off on some of the monitoring equipment: *ding ding ding ding ding*! Looking back on it now, I believe the stroke occurred then and there while the Rav lay in the ambulance. When we finally got to an emergency room that would take us, he was so disoriented he couldn't answer the usual questions about the date or the name of the current president.

The ER doctor turned to the triage nurse who was assisting him and said, "We have to admit this man. I think he's had a stroke."

"A stroke?" I responded in disbelief. "No, he's hallucinating because he's got a high fever. He had some kind of abdominal attack. I think it's pancreatitis."

By the time they got the Rav into a bed at the ER, he was completely unresponsive. They wheeled him out for a battery of tests. After what seemed an eternity, they brought the Rav's gurney back into the curtained cubicle where I'd been waiting. The doctor now had a diagnosis for me. "You're right," he said. "Your husband does have pancreatitis. But he also had a stroke."

After analyzing his brain scans, a neurologist came into the cubicle to examine the Rav. "This is a very, very sick man," he said shaking his head. "He has had a brainstem stroke. I am sorry to tell you he may not survive. But if he does, he may stay in a comatose state for the rest of his life. The brainstem has sustained a great deal of damage."

It later turned out that this diagnosis was incorrect. In fact, it was a frontal lobe stroke. Either way, it was devastating news, yet for some reason, I didn't buy it. I thought back to the Rav's recent lecture and remembered his words: *It's only a test, do not be ashamed, do not to be afraid say, "No, no, I will not accept it."*

"No, no," I argued with the doctor. "Even if he has had a brainstem stroke, he's not going to die. He's going to live, and he's going to be fine." I knew the Rav better than anyone. I refused to accept what the neurologist had told me, not because I was in denial but because I knew who was lying in that hospital bed.

Deep in my soul I felt that the Rav was not a victim of circumstance. Strokes are not random occurrences. No disease is. He took on this fight willingly to serve as an example of mind triumphing over matter. As the Rav himself had described it, *"The body can heal itself of all sickness and disease at the most fundamental level of reality, including our atoms, the subatomic particles that produce an atom, and far beyond that."*

I called Yehuda and Michael, who jumped on a small plane with a friend and flew to Las Vegas in a flash. On Friday afternoon, a few other close friends rushed to the hospital from Los Angeles to be with our family so we could have at least 10 people for Shabbat. If anything could pull the Rav out of this situation, we thought that it would be the energy of the Sabbath. There was no way the Rav would miss it.

As the Rav lay motionless in the room with our friends surrounding us, my confidence was shaken. It was painful to see the powerful, loving, larger-than-life man I loved look so frail and helpless. I cried many times that afternoon, yet I was also distracted by concerns that our friends be comfortable. In that way, at least, the moment felt familiar; even when things were most difficult, I had to take care of the people around me. That's how the Light set it up.

I stationed myself on the closed toilet seat in the lavatory for hours, looking through its open door at the rest of the room so our friends could sit around the Rav's bed. They opened his eyelids but his gaze was absent. It was a frightening sight, although a warm glow still radiated from his face.

As the sun began to set and the energy of Shabbat permeated the room, we started to sing Lecha Dodi, the hymn that has the power to draw down the energy of the Shabbat bride, the female aspect of the Creator. It was the hardest Lecha Dodi our family had ever sung. As we began. I watched my sons burst into uncontrollable tears. And then suddenly, in the middle of this haunting ancient melody, something shifted. The mood in the room inexplicably elevated, although nothing in the Rav's condition seemed to have changed.

The doctors were quite sure that that my husband would remain unconscious. His scans showed terrible brain damage. But later that night, around three in the morning, the Rav's right hand stirred. He was trying to glide it over his body, a kabbalistic technique of healing he had used daily and had taught our students around the world. Then his mouth began moving. He was whispering, mumbling, and then suddenly he recited a prayer. A minute later, all of us were accompanying him as he sang Lecha Dodi.

Electricity filled the room. We opened the Rav's eyelids but his stare still seemed vacant. He was unconscious, yet he sang every word of the song. How was that possible? All of us remained convinced that the Rav would make a miracle occur, and he would do so before Shabbat ended at sundown on Saturday night. But through the rest of the night and all day Saturday, the Rav lay unconscious as doctors and nurses came in and out of the room to monitor his condition.

The Rav's favorite part of Shabbat has always been the Third Meal, which takes place late Saturday afternoon. It's a profound time of healing, a moment to draw down power to fortify the immune systems of the body and the world. The Rav taught that Third Meal energy is also about the Final Redemption of humankind. It was during the Third Meal that our friend, neurosurgeon David Baskin, flew in from Houston to visit the Rav. He pressed the Rav's big toe, and in response, the Rav did something quite spectacular. Without warning, my husband opened his eyes.

We put a Kiddush cup in his hands, and he was able to partially recite the blessing over the wine—with his eyes wide open. When he finished, he drifted back to wherever it was he went in his semi-comatose state. But we all knew that somehow the Rav was in control. Given the odds, he should not have woken up. He should not have prayed or sung. In fact, he should not have survived this devastating stroke! And yet, there he was, doing all of these very things.

Later that night, the Rav started to sing again. Actually, his voice became so loud that the staff had to wheel his bed to the end of the ICU so he wouldn't disturb the rest of the very sick people there. One of the doctors on staff, a cardiologist who was monitoring the Rav's heart, pulled aside a Kabbalah student and dear friend, the late Artur Spokojny, and expressed his utter amazement. He demanded to know who that man was lying in the bed and asked Artur to send information about him. I don't know if Artur ever did but this was the kind of thing that happened all the time with the Rav. Even in this terribly compromised state he was making his usual powerful impression on people.

Over the next few days, my mind was in a thousand places. The Rav's stroke didn't mean that the work of the Kabbalah Centre could grind to a halt. It was September 15th, only two weeks away was Rosh Hashanah. We had been planning to celebrate the holiday in Israel—something we hadn't done since the early days, and a group of almost 3,000 students from all round the world was planning to congregate there. The strangest thing was that before the trip, I kept on saying, "No, we're not going to Israel. I don't know why we're making plans!" Somehow I knew that it wasn't going to happen.

After the stroke, Madonna called me. "What do you want me to do?" she asked. "How can I support you?"

"We're not going to Israel," I told her. "None of our family will be there. I'm worried about all the people who are traveling there to experience Rosh Hashanah with the Rav. It's just not right to cancel when they've already made arrangements and booked flights and hotels."

Madonna flew to Israel for Rosh Hashanah to join the 3,000 others who would show up. Eitan Yardeni, supported by many of our teachers, led the event. We had told the entire group about the stroke by video and encouraged everyone to use the tools and connect to the teachings not the teacher. And everyone stepped up, heart and soul. It was incredible. Although it was thousands of miles away, there's no question that their energy sustained the Rav.

While preparations were taking place in Israel, I was still struggling in Las Vegas. I don't recall how long we spent in that hospital—maybe a week or ten days. When the Rav's condition stabilized, we transferred him by Medevac to UCLA Hospital in West Los Angeles. He spent Yom Kippur there. By Sukkot, five days later, we moved him to Cedars-Sinai Medical Center where he remained for a good two months. During all that time, he didn't speak unless the doctors put a phone up to his ear. Then he would say yes, or no. Otherwise he just sat and stared.

How did I react? I had so many conflicting feelings. First of all, I was hopeful. My husband was still here, right in front of me. Still, I didn't know what was going to happen. The situation was certainly dire. He was very sick, yet he was no typical patient. The doctors had told us that rehabilitation would take eighteen months, and a lot could happen in that time, both good and bad.

I was in a lot of pain. I knew that whatever happened, our lives would never be the same. And I hated that history was repeating itself. The Rav's father had a medical emergency during a holiday and he didn't go to the hospital because he refused to travel on that day. He died. Rav Brandwein stopped taking his blood thinning medicine because it wasn't Kosher for Passover and he had a heart attack on the third day of Pesach. The Rav's stubbornness in refusing blood thinners may have led to his stroke, so among the many raw emotions running through me during that time was anger. Had he taken the medication, maybe this would not have happened.

On the other hand, the outcome might have been worse because blood thinners can cause profuse bleeding. I just don't know, and I never will. I only have certainty that this was part of the Creator's plan.

Over time, the Rav's condition improved. He was still not the person we had known, and he presented many challenges to me especially, but he was definitely not unresponsive. A year later, the Rav even delivered a brief lecture during a big Kabbalah Centre event. When he finished, Dr. Baskin, the neurologist who had come from Houston to visit the Rav that day in Vegas, stood up in front of 2,000 people and said that based on the damage to the Rav's brain what he had just done was a physical impossibility. The Rav began speaking more often at big events like this one, and even on Shabbat once in a while, as well as performing ceremonies like weddings and baby namings. Medical science simply could not account for the Rav's improved status. He could, however. A student at the Centre who was friends with the Rav once asked him how he could function so well after such a devastating brain injury. How was the Rav able to do what he was doing? The Rav told him something beautiful. "The DNA found in the leaf of the lemon is the very same DNA found in the fruit," he said. "Although the cells in my brain were destroyed, I can still access consciousness from the other cells in my body to perform these functions. I re-wired my body's process."

What a remarkable statement for any man to make, let alone a man who has suffered a massive stroke!

* * *

A year before his medical event in Las Vegas, the Rav started writing a revolutionary book entitled Nano: The Technology of Mind over Matter. It was published with the help of our son Yehuda in 2008. The Rav was excited by the new science of nanotechnology because in it he found language and concepts he could use to convey some of the most important aspects of kabbalistic wisdom. Nanoscience—the study of extremely small things—offers us the opportunity to intervene in the human body at the level of individual molecules.

The way nanotechnologists describe how to reach such grand goals as endless biological repairs—and therefore immortality—mirrors ideas laid out in the Zohar thousands of years ago. What had been missing until now was a way to draw these parallels in a way that would be understandable to the average person. This was the Rav's purpose in writing the book. He planned to publish it in the winter of 2004. Instead of writing these concepts, the Rav would live them.

Kabbalists are teachers, but they don't just disseminate information. They often become channels that embody all that they share. They teach by living example. We can see the truth of this in the Rav's life up until this point. From the moment he met Rav Brandwein, my husband did everything in his power to live the principles he taught. He buried one child and was rejected by others; he lost a fortune and political power; he was humbled by years of knocking on doors that slammed in his face. He endured slander and persecution by his very own community, friends, and family. His ego was trampled. Yet all this only served to make him stronger and more determined. It gave him greater clarity and certainty in the work that he was doing. It made him the Rav.

In 1984, when the Kabbalah Centre in Israel was booming, he watched our closest Chevre turn on him and walk away to disseminate a more Orthodox version of Kabbalah. This taught him the importance of giving unconditionally, of expecting nothing in return for the love, and of answering rejection with even more love.

The Rav slept just a few hours a night every night of the week for at least twenty years. As the Kabbalah Centre expanded around the world, he helped solve the problems of the Chevre and students living in faraway lands as well as around the corner. Their pain was his pain, their struggles his. He would not abandon them, no matter what the cost to himself. What's more, he would use the opportunity of this stroke to teach us all how to exert the strength of our spirit to overcome the illusion of physicality.

With his stroke the Rav took it upon himself to destroy the root of chaos, disease, and death. He was driven by the belief that if not his generation, perhaps the next one, or the one after that could reach a critical mass of Light and energy, banishing chaos and overcoming death.

The Zohar teaches that we don't live forever right now because of the opponent, Satan, the force of darkness, so we can become the cause and reason of revealing the Light.

Right now, the Light inside us is limited by the confines of the body. But if humanity as a whole could reach a higher plane through spiritual awakening, the amount of Light released would illuminate every nook and cranny of this physical world. This is what we call *Mashiach*, the Messiah. Death and the illusion of this world would no longer be necessary. Humankind would have fulfilled its destiny and with that become immortal.

Looking at the world today it's difficult not to focus on how much darkness exists, yet the Rav knew that you can't fix the darkness. His message was to add more Light. When a room is dark, you flip a switch or turn on a lamp.

* * *

After the stroke, my husband stayed with us for nine more years. I believe he did so through sheer force of will. He knew that if he had left us immediately on September 2, 2004, everything he had created would have collapsed. Too much of the work rested on his shoulders alone. The Rav had been able to change the energy in a room simply by entering it. No wonder he had exhorted the group gathered on that Shabbat a few weeks before the stroke to "become the Rav." He now risked everything he had—life itself—to ensure that others would take over so that the Kabbalah Centre and its teachings could continue to grow and flourish in his absence.

So began a long period of transition. The Rav faded in and out but he continued to participate at the Centre. People still saw and interacted with him on a limited basis. He would make Kiddush on Friday nights. He would sing and say prayers. He would sit quietly in a corner and observe. Sometimes he would rock and mumble, and at other times, to everyone's astonishment, he would fully show up. Those moments took our collective breath away.

He remained engaged as long as someone needed him, and then a few moments later he would shut down and turn inward once more. Although much of the time he spoke gibberish, on other occasions he gave lectures that were shocking in their clarity and insight; he had achieved a high degree of prophecy, tapping into future events. But these moments became fewer and farther between as years passed.

At first, the Rav couldn't walk unsupported, so we found a helper to take care of him. We introduced him to every therapy you can imagine: we put him in a hyperbaric chamber; we tried acupuncture; we tried anything and everything that could be done. Eventually the Rav learned to walk with assistance.

At the request of our friend Dr. Baskin, we took the Rav to Houston one year after the stroke to see if there was anything more we could do for him. After a young physician conducted a pre-examination he said, "I think you brought the wrong scans with you. Your husband is walking and communicating. He's part of a community. That would be impossible according to these tests. If they are the right scans, then he must have rewired his brain somehow."

Research shows that the brain has a quality called neuroplasticity, which allows it to create new connections to compensate for damaged areas. Certainly, there is a lot we still don't know about how this miraculous organ works.

For the Chevre, other members of the Centre, and students, the Rav's state was a mixed bag. He was out of touch sometimes, but totally with it and even loving at others. But that love did not seem to extend to me.

After the stroke, the Rav expressed lots of emotions—he yelled, he was angry, he was subdued, he was withdrawn—but he no longer expressed tenderness toward me. As far as I could tell, the affection we'd shared all of our lives was gone. If I walked in the room and said, "Hi" to him, he offered no response. Nor did this change. Our interactions went in one direction only. In fact, if he was spending time with other people and I came by, his mood would suddenly sour. Sometimes he would yell at me, "Go away! Leave me alone." This was so painful I even took to living in a different house for a while.

Once, out of frustration, I shouted at him, "Why the hell did you do this? Why did you have a stroke? You're a Leo! Why couln't you have had an honest to goodness heart attack?"

His response: "I'm on vacation, remember? I'm on vacation." I didn't know what to say.

Other than that, he almost never spoke to me. Others reported that in his moments of clarity he spoke the kindest and most thoughtful words to them. But never to me or to our sons. It was maddening. What was the Creator trying to teach us with this trial? I couldn't fathom it.

Eventually, however, years into our new lives, rumors started to reach me that the Rav had a calculated reason for pushing his family away. He didn't share these thoughts with his inner circle but to a lawyer who represented us and an educator who was helping the Centre design a new curriculum. The educator's story, in particular, was so fascinating that I'm including it here.

I had been working for the Centre for maybe three weeks. The Rav would be there sometimes, just sitting in a corner either mumbling in Hebrew, rocking back and forth in his chair or saying nonsensical things. When I first encountered him, I asked "Should I do anything for him?"

I was told, No. That's just the way he is. He's fine. He likes being here."

On this one occasion, maybe my third or fourth work session, the Rav sat in a corner, as usual. But this time, once we were alone the Rav stood up and walked over. He looked at me and said, "Do you know why I brought you here?"

"Rav," I replied, astonished by this sudden change. "I was hired to work on the lessons."

He looked at me with a little smile. Then he said, "The reason I brought you here is very important. I'm going to share some things you need to remember. But first, may I give you a blessing?"

The Rav was totally lucid and coherent, as if nothing were wrong with him. He walked around behind my chair, put his hands on my head, and began saying a prayer in Hebrew. I started to cry uncontrollably; I could feel energy all around the room and in my body. I now understood what I had heard so many times—that you can feel the strength of his energy through his touch.

When he was finished with the prayer, the Rav came back around and said, "I'm going to share a few things with you now. The reason I chose to leave this way—with a stroke—I want you to be clear that this was not an accident. I chose this so I could leave slowly. That way, people can adapt, they can get ready. If I'd left right away, the Centre would go away, and all the work we've done would disappear."

When we heard someone approaching, he said. "Now they are coming back so I'm going to sit down." He returned to his chair as if nothing had happened, started rocking and mumbling again.

This happened several times. When it did, I saw that this man still had dominion over his body. I had no doubt that he chose how he presented himself. At some point, I arranged to see his brain scans and talk to his neurologist. He told me what I already knew, that the Rav shouldn't have been able to carry on a lucid conversation, yet sometimes he was totally there, as if he'd never had the stroke.

A couple of years later, I was at the Rav and Karen's house, working with Karen on some content for her upcoming book tour. She got busy with something else, and the Rav's caregiver told me that he wanted to talk to me. I went to see him. He was lucid again.

"Karen doesn't understand why I yell at her, why I appear angry with her all the time and push her away," he said. "It's because our love is the greatest gift the Creator gave us. We're so bonded. But Karen is so loyal to our love that if I showed her even one time that I could come back like I'm

doing with you, she would never leave my side. She would not do her sacred work. Instead she would be waiting for the next connection with me. So I shun her whenever she's around. This is the most painful thing I've ever had to do," the Rav continued, "because I love her more than anything in the world. And I'm telling you this because there will come a time when you'll need to share it with my beloved."

"How will I know when it's time?" I asked.

"I'll come to you," the Rav said. He gave me a blessing, and I left.

Several years later, this educator did share the Rav's words with me in a Japanese garden. It was heartbreaking, beautiful, and amazing.

* * *

Around 2007, we started thinking about a burial site for the Rav. Once again, I had to deal with the practical aspects of the situation. He was nearing 80, he'd had a debilitating stroke, and now he had developed frontal lobe dementia, where the part of the brain that makes executive decisions begins to deteriorate. Symptoms include difficulties with language and argumentativeness (especially with loved ones); changes in behavior like tactlessness, passivity, lack of motivation, pacing, and wandering. I'd certainly seen some of these in the Rav's behavior. This is a slow degenerative process; life expectancy ranges from two to ten years.

That year, I realized that it was time to create a final resting place for the Rav. I went to Israel and traveled around with some friends in search of a cemetery or an area adjacent to a holy site or cemetery where we could buy a significant piece of land. We looked in Jerusalem but could only find individual plots. I knew that many of our Chevre and students—potentially hundreds of people at a time—would want to visit the Rav's grave after he transitioned, so these were too small.

Eventually we journeyed north to the city of Safed, one of Judaism's Four Holy Cities. At the foot of a mountain in the same ancient cemetery where the Ari is buried, we found a parcel that consisted of thirty-six adjoining burial plots. So we acquired it. Our sons then oversaw the construction of a specially designed burial chamber dug into a cave. They dealt with the Chief Rabbi of Safed and were required to adhere to the restrictions he imposed.

Our primary concern became keeping this project under wraps. First of all, even though I'd said, "Let's do this," I still felt pretty conflicted about it. I asked myself, "If we prepare this grave in advance, are we hastening the Rav's death?" This was a spiritual matter. After searching through the kabbalistic texts, we found a teaching that explained: "Contemplating the fact that our days on this plane are numbered helps us consciously evolve. If you prepare a plot during a person's lifetime, it may extend his or her life." I was calmed by this.

Still, almost no one knew about the project except for me, our sons, the builders, and a few individuals directly involved in it. Two donors were gracious enough to help us with the financing, as this tomb was a big undertaking. We needed to make sure their funds didn't co-mingle with those of the Centre. If we had to go through our board, lawyers, and accountants the whole world would have learned about the construction—something we wanted to avoid. I was adamant that the ultra-Orthodox establishment in Israel, with the exception of the Chief Rabbi of Safed, be kept out of the loop.

Yehoshua, one of the Rav's sons from his marriage to Rivka (we call him Shuy), later told us a story that while the tomb was under construction, a friend who lived in Safed went to the cemetery to see what was being built there. The town had been buzzing about it since it was much larger and more elaborate than an ordinary grave. While Shuy's friend was there, he saw a snake guarding the entry. He knew immediately that a special person was going to be buried there.

After the grave was completed, we kept it ready. It remained empty for six more years.

* * *

Shuy came into our lives after the Rav's stroke. He began calling from Brooklyn every Friday afternoon to wish his father Shabbat Shalom. Several times, he flew to Los Angeles with his brother, Naftali, just to spend Shabbat with their father. His active engagement delighted us, but it was also puzzling after so many years of estrangement. One day, Yehuda said to him, "We're happy that you're spending time with the Rav after all these years. We just want to understand why."

Shuy responded with a story. One of his sons, the Rav's grandson, longed for a large family but he and his wife were having difficulty getting pregnant. Shuy went to his Rebbe to ask for a blessing for his son so that his daughter-in-law could conceive. But rather than giving the blessing, the Rebbe posed Shuy a question. "What about honoring your father?" Shuy came to Los Angeles, the Rav gave him a blessing, and sure enough, his daughter-in-law became pregnant. From that moment on, Shuy spoke to and visited his father as much as he could.

* * *

At the age of seventy, it's traditional to start counting the years of one's life again as if from the beginning. This isn't a kabbalistic principle, Orthodox people do it as well. When a man reaches the age of 83, it's time for him to have a second Bar Mitzvah. For the Rav we decided to throw a big birthday party in Jerusalem in a venue adjacent to the Old City. Actor Ashton Kutcher spoke about how the Rav, with a simple question, had inspired him to open Thorn, a foundation that uses modern technology to fight child trafficking, pornography, and sexual abuse. This was the effect the Rav had on people.

Coincidentally, one of Shuy's children was getting married in Israel at the same time, inspiring a big family reunion that included a large number of the Rav's children, grandchildren and great-grandchildren. Naftali had to fly home early but his older siblings decided to spend some time with their father. Shuy, in particular, later reported that he had had a very good conversation with the Rav. They spoke about old times, and some healing took place. It was a wonderful time for all of us.

* * *

Before the stroke, with Los Angeles as our home base, the Rav and I had been spending two to three months each year flying back and forth between New York, Israel, and Los Angeles, with some other Centres sprinkled in for good measure. Following the stroke, I began to travel on my own, leaving the Rav in Los Angeles. In 2012, a group of teachers wanted the Rav to visit as many Centres around the globe as possible while he still could. Some of them started planning the trip without my knowledge. "The Rav has so much to offer our students," they reasoned. "He shouldn't sit around at home."

I felt the Rav was not up for such a strenuous journey, and I was quite upset that this planning was taking place without consulting me. On the other hand, our community had continued to expand during these years when the Rav was partially incapacitated. The wisdom itself, the passion of our teachers and students, and word-of-mouth had extended Kabbalah's influence throughout the world. Many of these people had never experienced the Rav first-hand, and they would certainly benefit from doing so.

So even though I argued against it, the Rav, his caregiver, and an entourage spent three months traveling to New York, Miami, Boca Raton, Canada, Russia, London, and Israel. Then, after a short breather, they spent another three months in Mexico, Panama, Colombia, Brazil, Argentina, and Venezuela. Given his fragile health, the Rav was taking a risk with such an ambitious schedule but the teachers thought it was important for the people and for the Rav. Many Kabbalah students would never be able to make a trip to the United States so this might be the only time they would see the Rav.

Despite my belief that he should not have gone, the Rav was able to create a beautiful connection in Caracas. Venezuela had been unsafe for a while, and the situation was deteriorating, so his teachers arranged for security to protect the Rav while he was there. A detail picked him up from the airport and brought him to the hotel, and guards were posted outside his room. Whenever the Rav went out, a security team accompanied him, along with students from the Caracas Centre.

Every afternoon, the Rav took a walk in a park near the hotel. He enjoyed the exercise, although he couldn't walk unassisted. Usually several Centre teachers with whom he felt very close would support him on either side but on this day when the teachers stepped forward, the Rav said, "No, no, no. Let Edgard take me."

Edgard was the head of the security detail, a big, burly man with a permanent scowl that inspired fear in anyone who looked at him. Edgard took the Rav's arm, and the two of them walked together, while the rest of the group trailed along behind. When they returned to the hotel, the Rav was about to go into his room when he stopped. He turned to Edgard and without saying a word, kissed him on the cheek. Then he retired.

We found out later that this unexpected act of love surprised Edgard and shook him to the core. He went back to his quarters and wept like a child. The next day, the Rav was leaving Caracas to continue his journey, and Edgard drove the group to the airport. He silently handed the Rav a neatly typed note in Spanish, translated here.

> *Last night after I helped you walk, you kissed me on the cheek. I felt something I had never felt in my entire life. I broke into tears when I went back into my room, recalling all the times I had acted in an arrogant or wrongful manner. That kiss changed something inside me. You are a saint, and from the bottom of my heart I can say that I am very proud to be by your side, even just for a moment in my life. I would give my life for you because of the love you feel for all of us. Thank you.*
>
> *—Edgard*

* * *

The Rav fell twice during these trips, which may have hastened his departure from this physical plane. By the late summer of 2013, it became obvious that his life expectancy was now a matter of days or weeks, not months or years. He was in and out of the ICU at Cedars-Sinai, and we all knew that the end was near.

In the Jewish faith, there is a ritual process for the body from the time the soul leaves it until it goes into the ground. This is called *tahara*, which means "cleansing." Our sons began researching the proper *tahara* for a kabbalist. We sent out feelers to different Orthodox groups to learn about their burial customs. The Grand Rabbi of Vizhnitz, who had been the leader of a Chassidic dynasty, had died six months earlier, so we contacted the man in charge of his final preparations and benefited from his advice.

Miraculously, we also found someone who had attended Rav Ashlag's funeral in 1954. He was elderly but his intellect was remarkably sharp, and he generously supplied many other intimate details. We made a list of the options we'd collected and found a good moment to speak to the Rav so we could also include his own desires.

A week or so before the Rav passed, Michael brought his son David, our grandson, to the hospital. The Rav roused himself, recognized them, and asked the child, "Will you be a *tzadik*?" Will you be a righteous person?" He called the boy "King David," and then went on to give him a blessing. It was such a special visit.

Our other son, Yehuda, went to the hospital every day after he finished his own prayers so he could pray with the

Rav. He brought a Shofar into the hospital room and blew it, as is traditional during the month of Elul, which leads up to Rosh Hashanah. The Rav was awake and participated as best he could. On September 2, however, the Rav became unresponsive. He did not return to us again.

The Rav passed on the 12th day of the month of Tishrei 5774, two days after Yom Kippur. This date corresponds to September 16, 2013 in the secular calendar, nine years to the day when 3,000 people prayed for the Rav in Israel. Did all those prayers give us nine more years with him?

Although his caregiver and the hospital staff were attending to the Rav, no one in the family was at his bedside the moment he left this plane. The nature of organ failure is such that it is very difficult to predict. My sons and I had been with the Rav almost continuously since we knew the end was near but he chose to leave us when we took a short break. On learning that his death was imminent, we hurried back, only to arrive minutes after he took his last breath. Although missing the moment of his transition was not easy, we understood that it was meant to be this way, just as it had been for the Rav with Rav Brandwein.

We all said our goodbyes. It was a Monday, the day we read from the Torah in the morning. Yehuda read the weekly portion for the Rav after his passing, and we could feel that his soul was still with us. It was a strangely peaceful moment.

Shortly thereafter, however, the hospital's administrative machinery kicked in. Medical procedures had to be charted and documents signed as to the exact time and cause of death. It felt surreal. Several students came in to say goodbye. The Rav's body remained in the hospital bed for a few hours before we could transport him.

Then our focus turned to arranging the funeral.

We had the Rav's body taken to the Centre and laid him in the War Room, the name he had given our sanctuary, surrounded by lit candles. Our Chevre, close friends, and students came and kept vigil, which gave them a chance to pray and connect to him. No one spoke, though Psalms were read. When the soul leaves and only the body remains, it is particularly susceptible to negative energies that can attach to it. The Psalms create a protective barrier.

Then we performed the *tahara*, (cleansing process). Some of our Chevre, along with a member of the Jewish Burial Society, came to wash the body. Then we lowered it into the *mikvah* for purification. After the Rav's body was removed from the water, members of the family immersed as well.

As the oldest son, Yehuda had specific duties to perform. Even though the Rav was going to be buried in Israel, Yehuda placed soil from the Promised Land on his father's eyelids to help the soul elevate. Finally, the Rav was wrapped in a white linen shroud similar to a *kittel*, the white cotton robe that married Ashkenazi men wear on special occasions. It was tied with a sash fashioned into the Hebrew letter Shin. This letter represents *Shadai*, God's protective presence, which is also found on a mezuzah.

Why a Shin? When we're alive we have an invisible Shin on our foreheads. When the Angel of Death arrives, he changes the Shin into a Tav, which symbolizes death. The Shin on the sash reconnects the deceased person to life—eternal life. It eclipses the power of Tav created by the Angel of Death.

That evening, our Chevre, students, and friends in Los Angeles who weren't traveling to Israel with us came to the Centre to say goodbye. But before we could leave, we had to overcome a serious logistical obstacle. According to Jewish law, we needed to get the Rav's body to the burial site in Safed before Sukkot began at sundown—just two days away. However, EL AL doesn't fly on Holy Days, and certainly not between Yom Kippur and Sukkot. We would have to wait five days, which was simply not possible.

So we turned to our friends, and through their generosity, we were able to transport the Rav in a large private plane that took all of us to Israel before the deadline. Thank you!

The Rav used to say that Lag B'Omer, the day commemorating Rav Shimon bar Yochai's passing, should be a day of celebration. Sorrow would seem appropriate when a person dies, but if you believe they've accomplished what they came into this world to do, then the day their soul is being released from its physical form and elevating calls for jubilation. Not only did the Rav's soul leave at an opportune moment, he himself had encouraged us to see his passing as a time for rejoicing. He had been very specific about it. "Don't mourn me when I pass. Make it a time of enlightenment."

Before the plane touched down in Israel, we all changed into white clothing. On our way to the cemetery in Safed, we made a little detour to take the Rav's body to the Idra Cave where Rav Shimon had revealed the Zohar to the world 2,000 years earlier. Kabbalists pray as they walk around a body seven times to help the soul elevate, so we performed this ritual at this sacred site.

As more and more of our Kabbalah Centre students began arriving, we transported the Rav's body to the prepared grave at the cemetery in Safed. Technically, our sons couldn't participate as pallbearers in the procession that brought the Rav to his final resting place because they were his children. So they arrived first and waited for the rest of us to come. In the meantime, the Jewish Burial Society in Israel confirmed that the cleansing measures taken in the States were performed correctly. By the time I showed up, roughly one thousand people had gathered at the burial place, including a few men in black whom we recognized as the Rav's children and grandchildren from his marriage to Rivka.

Once everyone was assembled, we recited prayers of forgiveness for the living and for the Rav. Since his death occurred in the month of Tishrei between Yom Kippur and Sukkot, we also recited the prayers traditionally spoken at this time.

While we were celebrating the Rav's elevation, bedlam broke out in the ultra-Orthodox community in Safed. People there were furious that we had built this tomb for the Rav in the Holy Land. We had been right to keep the construction of the tomb a secret but now that the news was public, it was though we had kicked over a hornet's nest. Even after all these years, feelings still ran high.

For the most part, the service for the Rav proceeded smoothly. Countless glowing, heartfelt speeches celebrated the Rav's life and achievements. My sons delivered their eulogies, but when I got up to do the same, some ultra-Orthodox men cut the power to the microphone so I couldn't be heard, which created an uproar. It's not that they disapproved of me as the Rav's wife, we were breaking the ultra-Orthodox rule prohibiting women from delivering eulogies at funerals. Fortunately, the police arrived to keep the peace.

After the entombment, we sat on the ground at the gravesite for about twenty minutes. That constituted our Shiva. It was all we had, since the traditional seven day period of mourning is always superseded by a Holy Day, and Sukkot began at nightfall. So we returned to the Centre in Tel Aviv and began the Holiday. We enjoyed a week of festivities as old friends and new ones joined us to celebrate both this holy time and the Rav's life.

Once again, I could see his intention at work. Had he passed at any other time, those seven days would have been spent in mourning. Instead, well-wishers greeted us in a Sukkah, a place of joy and merriment. It is considered a *mitzvah*, a good deed, to be in the Sukkah for as many hours as possible, and even to sleep there. From a conventional Jewish perspective this serves as a reminder of our time in the desert, however, the Rav also taught us that the

Sukkah serves as our protective shield for the coming year. For those seven days we receive blessing for the coming year, and every moment in the Sukkah helps us gather more of that Light.

How different this occasion might have been. But seven days of mourning gave way to an outpouring of blessings and joy. Thank you Rav.

* * *

As his wife, I wish the Rav had remained on this plane a little longer. That said, I do understand that everything unfolded according to the Creator's plan—and the Rav's, as well. Today, we all have access to the Rav's soul in ways we could not when it was encased in a physical body. I no longer feel alone. His presence is part of me. His are the thoughts in my head and the words on my lips. Sometimes I find myself looking around and asking myself, *Who said that?* Then I realize, *Oh, you're here*. The Rav and I are soul mates. He has finished his job here; now it is my turn to complete this last stretch of the journey before I rejoin him.

* * *

Yom Kippur is such a significant moment. It is a time when the soul can draw down the abundance of the Sefira Binah—the storehouse of spiritual energy—into the physical world. The Rav called this unimaginable Light, Light beyond our wildest dreams. On Yom Kippur, a day free of Satan's energy, we are all cleansed and elevated to the level of the angels, unencumbered by the limitations of the physical realm. On Yom Kippur, the Rav fell into a coma from which he did not emerge. On Yom Kippur, he began his ascent, leaving behind the body that had provided his soul with a home to reveal its purpose.

That last Yom Kippur, Yehuda and a small group of friends came to the Rav's bedside to pray. They were there to celebrate Neilah, the final prayers of this Holy Day that signify the closing of the gates. This is the moment when our future is determined. Of course, the Rav would not be sealed in the Book of Life for one more year. His fate had already been decided; he would leave us two days later. But I remember how, exactly forty years earlier, the Rav had fought to observe the Neilah prayer in the middle of a war. How strong was his conviction, then, his power, his certainty. This is the lesson and the gift that his life gave to all of us.

And it is more than enough.

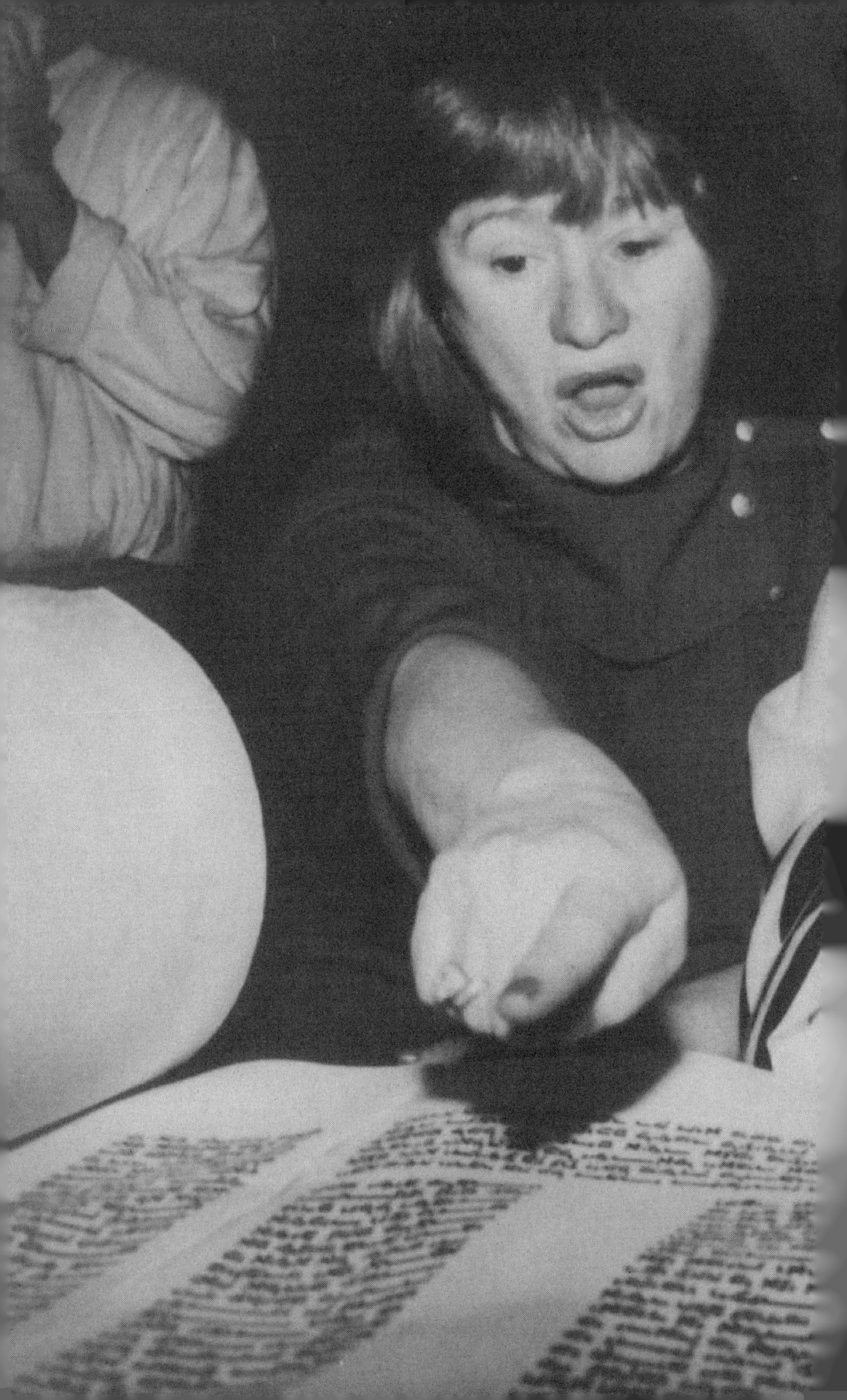

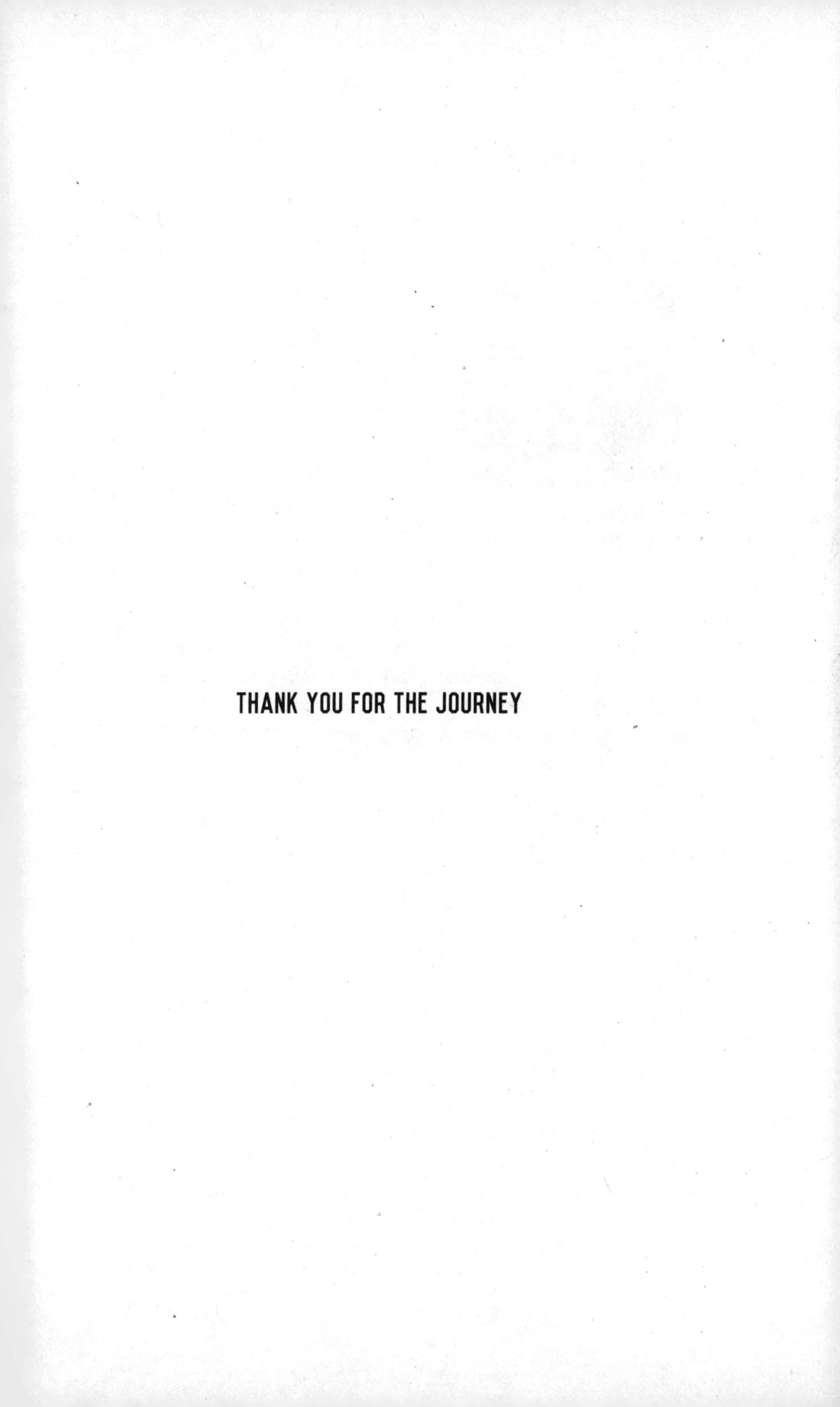
THANK YOU FOR THE JOURNEY

About the Author

Karen Berg
Founder, The Kabbalah Centre

"We can bring peace to this world and create real lasting change when we find a way to establish a binding of people based on the spark of the Creator that is within each of us."
—Karen Berg

Over four decades ago, Karen and her husband, Rav Berg, set out to make Kabbalah understandable and relevant to all people. Their goal was to teach the spiritual wisdom and tools of Kabbalah, without exclusion. They believed that learning Kabbalah could help people improve their lives, and that by doing so, the world would benefit. Under their leadership, The Kabbalah Centre has grown from a single location into one of the world's leading sources of spiritual wisdom, with more than 40 Centres around the globe that provide instruction and community to tens of thousands of students.

As the Founder of The Kabbalah Centre, Karen is devoted to an enduring vision—that within each person there is a spark of God that can be bound together to create transcendence beyond all differences.

Karen is certain that peace is possible and foresees a world free of hatred and intolerance. She works untiringly to cultivate a new paradigm of Global Spirituality in which people from diverse beliefs can work together to bring the world to a better place through mutual respect, dignity, and love for humanity.

To this end Karen has:

- Created the international children's program Spirituality for Kids (SFK), an online children's educational program that supports children in finding the spark of Light within themselves, within others, and within all things.

- Founded Kids Creating Peace (KCP), a program designed to help children discover for themselves a place of peaceful coexistence in the Middle East.

- Discussed human dignity and peace with many spiritual leaders including: His Holiness the Dalai Lama; Sri Sri Ravi Shankar, founder of the Art of Living Centres; Imam Mohammed Ali Elahi, Spiritual Leader of the Islamic House of Wisdom; Michael Bernard Beckwith, founder and CEO of the Agape Centre International; Bawa Jain, Secretary-General of the Millennium World Council of Religious Leaders; Mabel Katz, authority on the ancient Hawaiian healing method, Ho'oponopono; and Ilchi Lee, founder and developer of Brain Education and Dahn Yoga. Karen has also spoken with political and thought leaders including: President Mahmoud Abbas of the Palestinian National Authority and Hilary Rantisi, Director of the Middle East Initiative at Harvard University. In London in 2011, Karen spoke alongside Dr. Jehan Sadat, human rights activist and widow of former Egyptian President Anwar Sadat, and later that year, hosted an event in honor of International Women's Day with Ibtisam Mahameed, co-founder of the Women's Interfaith Encounter, and Professor Galia Sabar, chair of African Studies at Tel Aviv University, both recipients of the Dalai Lama Unsung Heroes of Compassion Award.

- Authored four groundbreaking works: Finding the Light Through the Darkness: Inspirational Lessons Rooted in the Bible and the Zohar; Simple Light: Wisdom from a Woman's Heart; To Be Continued: Reincarnation and the Purpose of our Lives; and Karen's first and most revolutionary title, God Wears Lipstick: Kabbalah for Women.

Following Rav Berg's passing in 2013, Karen continues to passionately lead and nurture Kabbalah Centres around the world. She has expanded her efforts to bring peace to the world through spiritual unity and travels extensively. Karen meets with people daily, both personally and online, serving a worldwide community of more than 300,000 souls. Karen has four children, sixteen grandchildren, and considers everywhere there is a Kabbalah Centre her home.

It is thanks to the support of donors that The Kabbalah Centre opens its doors and publishes its works.

The following sentiments were written by students whose financial support made the publication of this book possible.

My late husband, Dr. Artur Spokojny and I, had the merit not only to know and witness the soul mate relationship of the Rav and Karen, but to be introduced to each other by Karen and later, married by the Rav. Were it not for their incredible, mutual love of helping those in need, my dear Artur would not have lived beyond the sentence of his illness with such purpose and longevity. Furthermore, the miracles of our two daughters, Rachael (Kelly) and Miriam, could not have been possible without the Rav and Karen.

With eternal love and gratitude,
Melissa Spokojny

May the merit of the Rav and Karen and the Light they revealed help elevate the consciousness of all those who desire and will desire to follow the path of Kabbalah.

May the Endless Light and love shared by the Rav and Karen inspire me to become an even greater being of sharing and that I may soon earn the gift of my soul mate.

May the wisdom of this book elevate the soul of my father Meir ben Samuel

bring long life and prosperity to my sons
Hayim Vedat and his family, Binyamin Metin

my mother Denise,
my brother Sami and his family

May their lives be always blessed and close to the Light!

To the one and only Karen,

You opened up the world's heart to the wisdom of
Kabbalah and you shared it with
every soul no matter who they were or where they
came from or what they had done.

Thank you Karen and the Rav for never giving up so
that Kabbalah could reach all of us
and for continuously sharing your Light and Love with
all the people of the world.

May the wisdom of Kabbalah give us the strength to
continue doing our spiritual work with Certainty and
Love, even in those moments in our life where we do
not see the Light so clearly.

And may every person in the world come to know and
feel the Light and Love of the Creator in our time.

We teach Kabbalah, not as a scholarly study but as a way of creating a better life and a better world.

WHO WE ARE

The Kabbalah Centre is a non-profit organization that makes the principles of Kabbalah understandable and relevant to everyday life. The Kabbalah Centre teachers provide students with spiritual tools based on kabbalistic principles that students can then apply as they see fit to improve their own lives and by doing so, make the world better. The Centre was founded by Rav Yehuda Ashlag in 1922 and now spans the globe with brick-and-mortar locations in more than 40 cities as well as an extensive online presence. To learn more, visit www.kabbalah.com.

WHAT WE TEACH

There are five core principles:

- **Sharing:** Sharing is the purpose of life and the only way to truly receive fulfillment. When individuals share, they connect to the force of energy that Kabbalah calls the Light—the Infinite Source of Goodness, the Divine Force, the Creator. By sharing, one can overcome ego—the force of negativity.

- **Awareness and Balance of the Ego:** The ego is a voice inside that directs people to be selfish, narrow-minded, limited, addicted, hurtful, irresponsible, negative, angry, and hateful. The ego is a main source of problems because it allows us to believe that others are separate from us. It is the opposite of sharing and humility. The ego also has a positive side, as it motivates one to take action. It is up to each individual to choose whether they act for themselves or whether to also act in the well-being of others. It is important to be aware of one's ego and to balance the positives and negatives.

- **Existence of Spiritual Laws:** There are spiritual laws in the universe that affect people's lives. One of these is the Law of Cause and Effect: What one puts out is what one get back, or what we sow is what we reap.

- **We Are All One:** Every human being has within him- or herself a spark of the Creator that binds each and every person into one totality. This understanding informs us of the spiritual precept that every human being must be treated with dignity at all times, under any circumstances. Individually, everyone is responsible for war and poverty in all parts of the world and individuals can't enjoy true and lasting fulfillment as long as others are suffering.

- **Leaving Our Comfort Zone Can Create Miracles:** Becoming uncomfortable for the sake of helping others taps us into a spiritual dimension that ultimately brings Light and positivity to our lives.

HOW WE TEACH

Courses and Classes. On a daily basis, The Kabbalah Centre focuses on a variety of ways to help students learn the core kabbalistic principles. For example, The Centre develops courses, classes, online lectures, books, and audio products. Online courses and lectures are critical for students located around the world who want to study Kabbalah but don't have access to a Kabbalah Centre in their community. To learn more, visit www.ukabbalah.com.

Spiritual Services and Events. The Centre organizes and hosts a variety of weekly and monthly events and spiritual services where students can participate in lectures, meditation and share meals together. Some events are held through live streaming online. The Centre organizes spiritual retreats and tours to energy sites, which are places that have been closely touched by great kabbalists. For example, tours take place at locations where kabbalists may have studied or been buried, or where ancient texts like the *Zohar* were authored. International events provide students from all over the world with an opportunity to make connections to unique energy available at certain times of the year. At these events, students meet with other students, share experiences and build friendships.

Volunteering. In the spirit of Kabbalah's principles that emphasize sharing, The Centre provides a volunteer program so that students can participate in charitable initiatives, which includes sharing the wisdom of Kabbalah itself through a mentoring program. Every year, hundreds of student volunteers organize projects that benefit their communities such as feeding the homeless, cleaning beaches and visiting hospital patients.

One-on-One. The Kabbalah Centre seeks to ensure that each student is supported in his or her study. Teachers and mentors are part of the educational infrastructure that is available to students 24 hours a day, seven days a week.

Hundreds of teachers are available worldwide for students as well as a study program for their continued development. Study takes place in person, by phone, in study groups, through webinars, and even self-directed study in audio format or online. To learn more visit, www.ukabbalah.com.

Publishing. Each year, The Centre translates and publishes some of the most challenging kabbalistic texts for advanced scholars including the *Zohar*, *Writings of the Ari*, and the *Ten Luminous Emanations with Commentary*. Drawing from these sources The Kabbalah Centre publishes books yearly in more than 30 languages that are tailored for both beginner- and intermediate-level students and distributed around the world.

***Zohar* Project.** The *Zohar*, the primary text of kabbalistic wisdom, is a commentary on biblical and spiritual matters composed and compiled over 2000 years ago and is believed to be a source of Light. Kabbalists believe that when it is brought into areas of darkness and turmoil, the *Zohar* can create change and bring about improvement. The Kabbalah Centre's *Zohar* Project shares the *Zohar* in 30 countries by distributing free copies to organizations and individuals in recognition of their service to the community and to areas where there is danger. Since 2007, over 600,00 copies of the *Zohar* were donated to hospitals, embassies, places of worship, universities, not-for-profit organizations, emergency services, war zones, natural disaster locations, soldiers, pilots, government officials, medical professionals, humanitarian aid workers, and more.

Kabbalah Centre Books

72 Names of God, The: Technology for the Soul
72 Names of God for Kids, The: A Treasury of Timeless Wisdom
72 Names of God Meditation Book, The
And You Shall Choose Life: An Essay on Kabbalah, the Purpose of Life, and Our True Spiritual Work
AstrologiK: Kabbalistic Astrology Guide for Children
Becoming Like God: Kabbalah and Our Ultimate Destiny
Beloved of My Soul: Letters of Our Master and Teacher Rav Yehuda Tzvi Brandwein to His Beloved Student Kabbalist Rav Berg
Consciousness and the Cosmos (previously Star Connection)
Days of Connection: A Guide to Kabbalah's Holidays and New Moons
Days of Power Part 1
Days of Power Part 2
Dialing God: Daily Connection Book
Education of a Kabbalist
Energy of the Hebrew Letters, The (previously Power of the Aleph Beth Vols. 1 and 2)
Fear is Not an Option
Finding the Light Through the Darkness: Inspirational Lessons Rooted in the Bible and the Zohar
God Wears Lipstick: Kabbalah for Women
Holy Grail, The: A Manifesto on the Zohar
If You Don't Like Your Life, Change It!: Using Kabbalah to Rewrite the Movie of Your Life
Immortality: The Inevitability of Eternal Life
Kabbalah Connection, The: Preparing the Soul For Pesach
Kabbalah for the Layman
Kabbalah Method, The: The Bridge Between Science and the Soul, Physics and Fulfillment, Quantum and the Creator
Kabbalah on the Sabbath: Elevating Our Soul to the Light
Kabbalah: The Power To Change Everything
Kabbalistic Astrology: And the Meaning of Our Lives
Kabbalistic Bible: Genesis
Kabbalistic Bible: Exodus
Kabbalistic Bible: Leviticus

Kabbalistic Bible: Numbers
Kabbalistic Bible: Deuteronomy
Light of Wisdom: On Wisdom, Life, and Eternity
Miracles, Mysteries, and Prayer Volume 1
Miracles, Mysteries, and Prayer Volume 2
Nano: Technology of Mind over Matter
Navigating The Universe: A Roadmap for Understanding the Cosmic Influences that Shape Our Lives (previously Time Zones)
On World Peace: Two Essays by the Holy Kabbalist Rav Yehuda Ashlag
Path to the Light: Decoding the Bible with Kabbalah: Book of Beresheet Volume 1
Path to the Light: Decoding the Bible with Kabbalah: Book of Beresheet Volume 2
Path to the Light: Decoding the Bible with Kabbalah: Book of Beresheet Volume 3
Path to the Light: Decoding the Bible with Kabbalah: Book of Beresheet Volume 4
Prayer of the Kabbalist, The: The 42-Letter Name of God
Power of Kabbalah, The: 13 Principles to Overcome Challenges and Achieve Fulfillment
Rebooting: Defeating Depression with the Power of Kabbalah
Satan: An Autobiography
Secret, The: Unlocking the Source of Joy & Fulfillment
Secrets of the Bible: Teachings from Kabbalistic Masters
Secrets of the Zohar: Stories and Meditations to Awaken the Heart
Simple Light: Wisdom from a Woman's Heart
Shabbat Connections
Taming Chaos: Harnessing the Secret Codes of the Universe to Make Sense of Our Lives
Thought of Creation, The: On the Individual, Humanity, and Their Ultimate Perfection
To Be Continued: Reincarnation & the Purpose of Our Lives
To the Power of One
True Prosperity: How to Have Everything
Two Unlikely People to Change the World: A Memoir by Karen Berg
Vokabbalahry: Words of Wisdom for Kids to Live By
Way Of The Kabbalist, The: A User's Guide to Technology for the Soul

Well of Life: Kabbalistic Wisdom from a Depth of Knowledge
Wheels of a Soul: Kabbalah and Reincarnation
Wisdom of Truth, The: 12 Essays by the Holy Kabbalist Rav Yehuda Ashlag
Zohar, The